REVELATION UNRAVELED

A Clear View of Bible Prophecy

WILLIAM R. VILLANUEVA

Revelation Unraveled

Copyright © 1996 by William R. Villanueva
Copyright © 2009 by William R. Villanueva (second edition)

Solid Rock Publishing, PO Box 1332, Ramseur, NC 27316

Website: *www.revelationunraveled.com*

All rights reserved.

ISBN 978-0-578-02278-9

Scriptures quoted are from the *New American Standard Bible* unless otherwise noted. Copyright © 1960, 1962, 1963, 1971, 1972, 1973, 1975, 1977 by The Lockman Foundation. Used by permission.

Scripture quotations from *The Amplified Bible,* copyright © 1954, 1958, 1987 by The Lockman Foundation.

Cover design by John M. Havel

*"He who hath an ear to hear,
let him hear what the Spirit says to the
churches."*

Revelation 3:13

A Word from the Author

I wrote *Revelation Unraveled* back in 1996 as a result of years of study and what I believe to be a leading of the Lord. The book was received well and motivated many people to reassess their walk with God. Since that time, political and social events continue to confirm the explicit warnings I gave about the times that lie ahead for our nation and the world.

I decided to republish *Revelation Unraveled* in order to bring hope and encouragement to those who may be experiencing a sense of helplessness and despair as they see the world and its policy makers move us ever closer toward a New World Order. Jesus said, *"And ye shall know the truth, and the truth shall make you free."* I believe you will find His promise to be true.

I pray you take seriously the warnings contained in this book. If heeded, it will give you and your family a true and lasting hope during what are certain to be more troubling and chaotic times ahead.

— Ramseur, NC,
June 2009

Table of Contents

Introduction vii

Chapter 1 - The Origin and Identity of the Beast 1

Chapter 2 - The Mark of the Beast 25

Chapter 3 - The Seventy Weeks of Daniel 39

Chapter 4 - The Man of Sin Revealed 69

Chapter 5 - A Comparison of the Words of Christ 81

Chapter 6 - The Chronology of the End Times 101

Chapter 7 - Christ's Message to the Seven Churches 149

Epilogue 171

Appendix 173

Endnotes 179

Introduction

In this book, *Revelation Unraveled*, I would like to share with you the reasons why I believe cataclysmic times lie ahead for our planet. In essence, I believe that in the not too distant future we will see the transfer of power from Satan, who is the god of this world, to Jesus Christ, who is King of Kings over all of God's creation and universe. What is important to realize about this whole transformation is that Satan is not going to give up his power easily. There will be tremendous heartache and remorse from Christians and unbelievers alike when those who are steeped in "the world" and all it has to offer will have to "make or break" with their complacency and indifference to the true things of God.

We should be aware that throughout Jesus Christ's ministry He spoke of His eventual return to gather believers unto Himself and bring about judgment on mankind. You may even remember as a child in Sunday school or in church hearing teachings about "the tribulation," "antichrist," "end times," "Armageddon" and the like. All these words have gotten our attention at times about the future of the world and whether these topics in Scripture are in fact ever going to take place.

Today, the average Christian is so busy and engrossed with the affairs of this life that few Christians, if any, are taking the time to truly ponder and seek answers to the questions they ask themselves from time to time such as — "What is God's plan for the future?" "How are all these things I've heard about Christ's coming and the end of time actually going to come about?" These are fantastic, dynamic questions and because they are questions of eternity, they deserve our close attention and study.

Today, every Christian needs to realize the potent effect Adam and Eve's original sin had on mankind. It was their disobedience to God's command that brought about the horrible results that we see today — namely ultimate death to man, and dominion over the earth was handed over to Satan — God's archenemy. Ever since that act of rebellion on man's part, the world has been on a collision course between two spiritual entities. Man is left to choose who he will worship in life, the god of this world, who is Satan, or the God and Father of our Lord Jesus Christ, the one true God and creator of all mankind. Satan has purposely muddied the whole magnitude of this all important choice by getting man's attention diverted to other things in the world such as the attainment of "fulfillment" through material wealth, sensual pleasures, or through ideologies and religions that run contrary to God's revealed Word. It is this fundamental issue of who and what man chooses to worship in life which will determine whether they enjoy the blessings of life in eternity, or instead suffer eternal death by rejecting the saving and atoning blood of Christ. It is only through an accurate knowledge of God's Word — the Bible — that people today are going to be awakened from the spiritual slumber they are in and begin to perceive the many subtleties that Satan is employing in order to gain further worship by almost everyone in the world today.

In Genesis 3:15 and Isaiah 53:4-5, God gave a promise that a savior would come and redeem mankind. Jesus Christ fulfilled this promise. Old Testament prophecies also speak of a coming Messiah that will have victory over the nations of the world and ultimately restore God's kingdom on earth. Given that truth, why is it that during Christ's ministry Israel's most powerful spiritual leaders were blind to the reality of the Messiah's arrival even though Jesus did powerful miracles, signs, and teachings attesting to that fact? The Pharisees and Sadducees possessed a tremendous knowledge of the Scriptures but were blind to the spiritual reality of what was actually taking place before their eyes. Why is this? It is because they were too wrapped up in the physical trappings of their religion and their own egos. They were living the laws of their religion, but not the Word of God, so they missed seeing the spiritual side of life. Their spiritual blindness however did not alter the fact that Jesus Christ, the Savior of mankind, was in their midst and pronouncing judgment upon them because of their unbelief. I wonder if the same thing is happening today. Many ministers, though aware that Christ came to redeem man, seem oblivious to understanding God's ultimate plan as revealed in the Scriptures. Topics such as how God plans to judge the world and bring in everlasting righteousness are not widely taught or encouraged. In other words, many ministers are enjoying living their religion, but are not delving into what Scripture says will and must happen before the Lord Jesus Christ can return. This indifference makes them ignorant of the spiritual battle being waged around them, and thus makes them neglect their responsibility to warn their "flock" of the worldwide revealing of antichrist and the subsequent persecution of God's people. Each one of God's people needs to know and discover that the prophesies and references to God's plan are not buried away in Old Testament texts but are to be found close by in the New Testament in books such as the Gospel of Matthew, Mark, and Luke, Paul's epistles to the Thessalonians, Timothy, and of course, the book of Revelation written by the Apostle John. The book of Revelation, despite its reputation for being filled with symbolism, mystery, and subjects too crazy to be understood, is where God gives us an all encompassing view of how He plans to bring to pass the end of the world as we know it and then institute His wonderful and loving will for all eternity. The subjects brought up in the book of Revelation are the issues God's people and mankind in general need to know so they can get a saving knowledge of Jesus Christ before it is too late!

Do I believe the events one sees taking place in the world are written about in the book of Revelation? Absolutely. Do I believe the forces pushing for a more global economy and the whole "information highway" juggernaut have anything to do with what Revelation says about the future? Yes I do. What does the future hold? Are Christians just supposed to "hang around" and wait for the rapture to happen? Hardly. As we go deep into the book of Daniel and the book of Revelation, it is my belief that the days of playing church are over. Christians everywhere are going to have to start thinking seriously about whether or not their faith is real and whether or not they are willing to pay the price needed to stand for the one true God, because in the critical days ahead, Satan, the devil, who is our adversary, will be trying his best to seduce and deceive out of this world every last person he can before he meets his final defeat at the hands of Jesus Christ — the true King of Kings and Lord of Lords.

Chapter 1

The Origin and Identity of the Beast

When studying the Book of Daniel it is important to realize that the years between 626-539 BC were a dark time in Israel's history. Israel had been disobeying God for years and it resulted in Israel being carried off into captivity by the Babylonians. Even though it was a dark time for the soul of Israel there was still much light that was shed on their future by the prophet Daniel. We learn from the Bible that Daniel was captured as a young boy and taken to Babylon where he was raised, taught, and highly respected in the king's household because of the wisdom he displayed and the ability God gave him to understand visions and dreams. This can be read about in Daniel 1:17-20.

It was during Daniel's exile in Babylon that King Nebuchadnezzar had a troubling dream and Nebuchadnezzar wanted to know the meaning of it. He asked his wise men to not only tell him the dream he had, but also to interpret it for him, a request that the Chaldean magicians and sorcerers told him could not be done. Because of this, Nebuchadnezzar became furious and declared that all the wise men in Babylon must die — an order that included Daniel despite his innocence. As one reads the record, it says that with the help of prayer by Shadrach, Meshach, and Abednego, Daniel received the answer from God that he needed; he got the vision of the dream that King Nebuchadnezzar had had, along with the interpretation. The entire record is found in Daniel 2:16-28. We begin at Daniel 2:31 where Daniel starts to give King Nebuchadnezzar the news:

> *Daniel 2:31* You, O king, were looking and behold, there was a single great statue; that statue, which was large and of extraordinary splendor, was standing in front of you, and its appearance was awesome. *32* The head of that statue [was made] of fine gold, its breast and its arms of silver, its belly

and its thighs of bronze, *33* its legs of iron, its feet partly of iron and partly of clay. *34* You continued looking until a stone was cut out without hands, and it struck the statue on its feet of iron and clay, and crushed them. *35* Then the iron, the clay, the bronze, the silver and the gold were crushed all at the same time, and became like chaff from the summer threshing floors; and the wind carried them away so that not a trace of them was found. But the stone that struck the statue became a great mountain and filled the whole earth.

Daniel then gives the king the interpretation...

Daniel 2:36 This [was] the dream; now we shall tell its interpretation before the king. *37* You, O king, are the king of kings, to whom the God of heaven has given the kingdom, the power, the strength, and the glory; *38* and wherever the sons of men dwell, [or] the beasts of the field, or the birds of the sky, He has given [them] into your hand and has caused you to rule over them all. You are the head of gold. *39* And after you there will arise another kingdom inferior to you, then another third kingdom of bronze, which will rule over all the earth. *40* Then there will be a fourth kingdom as strong as iron; inasmuch as iron crushes and shatters all things, so, like iron that breaks in pieces, it will crush and break all these in pieces. *41* And in that you saw the feet and toes, partly of potter's clay and partly of iron, it will be a divided kingdom; but it will have in it the toughness of iron, inasmuch as you saw the iron mixed with common clay. *42* And [as] the toes of the feet [were] partly of iron and partly of pottery, [so] some of the kingdom will be strong and part of it will be brittle. *43* And in that you saw the iron mixed with common clay, they will combine with one another in the seed of men; but they will not adhere to one another, even as iron does not combine with pottery. *44* And in the days of those kings the God of heaven will set up a kingdom which will never be destroyed, and [that] kingdom will not be left for another people; it will crush and put an end to all these kingdoms, but it will itself endure forever. *45* Inasmuch as you saw that a stone was cut out of the mountain without hands and that it crushed the iron, the bronze, the clay, the silver, and the gold, the great God has made known to the king what will take place in the future; so the dream is true, and its interpretation is trustworthy.

What was Daniel talking about and how does it pertain to us today? First of all, in verses 37-38, it shows us that as egotistical and as pagan a king Nebuchadnezzar was, he was still put there by God. This is an important truth to remember especially when we begin to consider the rise of the "little horn" that precedes the final beast kingdom, the kingdom which will usher in the greatest conflict ever witnessed by man — the Great Tribulation and the Day of the Lord.

Daniel tells us that God made Nebuchadnezzar ruler over the world around him and that he was the statue's head of gold. After this kingdom of Babylon, another kingdom would arise, represented by the statue's breasts and two arms of silver — which we know historically and biblically to be the Medo-Persian Empire. We can see this fact verified from Daniel 5:28 where it describes a party that Nebuchadnezzar's son, Belshazzar, was hosting. During the party Belshazzar sinned by using special goblets from God's temple during the festivities. Because of this sin, God wrote a message on the wall telling Belshazzar that he would no longer be king, and the message reads in verse 28, *"PERES, Thy kingdom is divided, and given to the Medes and Persians."* Thus we see from Scripture itself that the next kingdom after Babylon was Medo-Persia.

Verse 32 of chapter 2 speaks of a third kingdom that has *"his belly and thighs of brass"* and according to verse 39 *"shall bear rule over all the earth."* When you study the chronology of world history, this part of the statue accurately represents Greece — specifically the rule of Alexander the Great, who before the age of thirty-three conquered the entire known world.

The fourth kingdom is categorized as "legs of iron" and is believed by virtually every Bible scholar to signify the Roman Empire. It is correctly shown as two legs or two kingdoms — the Western division being centered in Rome, and then the Eastern division, whose capital was Constantinople. In Daniel 2, verse 40 it says, *"Then there will be a fourth kingdom as strong as iron; in as much as iron crushes and shatters all things, so, like iron that breaks in pieces, it will crush and break all these in pieces."* This verse makes the point that Rome had tremendous strength and power toward everybody within its grasp.

REVELATION UNRAVELED

The accuracy of Nebuchadnezzar's dream and its interpretation by Daniel is remarkable because these kingdoms did come to pass and they came to pass in the exact order they were given. This being so, we need to remember that this dream and the interpretation were given to Nebuchadnezzar to explain what would happen *in the future*. Previous to Nebuchadnezzar's kingdom, there were two other great world powers that played a part in human history. The first kingdom was Egypt that we remember for its splendor and for the intelligence of its people. The second kingdom was that of Assyria which conquered the northern kingdom, comprised of ten of the twelve tribes of Israel. The Assyrians exiled the ten tribes into both Assyria and into the cities of the Medes, which one can read about in 2 Kings 17:6. When you take these two kingdoms, Egypt and Assyria, and couple them with the information given in Nebuchadnezzar's dream, you get a look at the history of the world that looks something like the chart below:

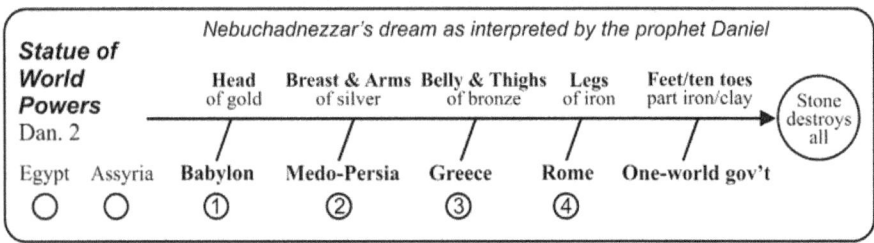

The chart categorizes Nebuchadnezzar's dream as it was interpreted by the prophet Daniel. The nations of Egypt and Assyria on the left will be discussed further in our study. As accurate as Daniel's description of the future is, we need to study in detail the last part of the statue, the feet and toes, so as to learn what implications lie ahead for *our* future. Daniel 2, verse 41:

> ***Daniel 2:41*** And in that you saw the feet and toes, partly of potter's clay and partly of iron, it will be a divided kingdom; but it will have in it the toughness of iron, inasmuch as you saw the iron mixed with common clay. ***42*** And [as] the toes of the feet [were] partly of iron and partly of pottery, [so] some of the kingdom will be strong and part of it will be brittle. ***43*** And in that you saw the iron mixed with common clay, they will combine with one another in the seed of men; but they will not adhere to one another, even as iron does not combine with pottery.

From what we have just read and as we look at the chronology of world empires, God says that after the Roman Empire will come another kingdom, partly made of *iron* (people made up of Roman descent or attributes) and partly made of *clay* (people of different nationalities and lesser strength). This final kingdom (singular — a very important point) will have the same awesome strength that the Roman Empire exhibited in past history, yet being "part clay" it will also be made up of other weaker nations. The phrase, "combined with one another in the seed of men" is saying, and it is confirmed throughout the Scriptures, that there will be an eventual creation of a one-world government. This is made perfectly clear in Revelation 17:12-13.

> **Revelation 17:12** And the ten horns which thou sawest are ten kings, which have received no kingdom as yet; but receive power as kings one hour with the beast. *13* These have one mind, and shall give their power and strength unto the beast. (KJV) (emphasis added)

From these verses we see that these ten kings are of one mind, and give their power and strength, all their resources, unto the beast — which is the book of Revelation's term for the coming one-world government. These kings will oversee ten "regions" yet serve and give their allegiance to the headquarters of the one-world government. The ten horns, or kings, had not received a kingdom as yet because the Apostle John was living during the time of the Roman Empire and this final kingdom of man, the feet with ten toes, had not yet come to pass.

Nebuchadnezzar's dream showed that a stone "cut out without hands," (i.e. wrought by God not by man) will shatter into pieces the feet made of iron and clay and then the nations that thrive under the banner of world government will be destroyed and become like chaff that is swept away by the wind. This "stone," which shatters all the kingdoms to pieces, then becomes a great mountain and fills the whole earth. Daniel explains this "stone" in verse 44...

> **Daniel 2:44** And in the day of those kings the God of heaven will set up a kingdom which will never be destroyed, and [that] kingdom will not be left for another people; it will crush and put an end to all these kingdoms, but it will itself endure forever.

Here we see God's plan. This "one-world" kingdom of man that is yet to appear, will in fact be the *last* kingdom before God sets up *His* kingdom, a kingdom that is going to supersede and consume all others because it will be a kingdom that shall never be destroyed but stand forever.

DANIEL SEVEN

We have seen from Daniel 2 that God was at work giving Daniel tremendous insight. Not only did God give Nebuchadnezzar a dream that unfolded the future of the world and its power structure in a succinct way, but He also revealed that prior to Christ's kingdom coming to pass, a world government would be formed and that it would have its roots in the Roman Empire. God did not stop there however, because in the visions that Daniel and the Apostle John received, God revealed even more details about these kingdoms, their ultimate destruction, and the ushering in of His everlasting kingdom.

In chapter seven of the book of Daniel we see that during the reign of Belshazzar, king of Babylon, Daniel himself had a dream.

> ***Daniel 7:3*** And four great beasts were coming up from the sea, different from one another. *4* The first [was] like a lion and had [the] wings of an eagle. I kept looking until its wings were plucked, and it was lifted up from the ground and made to stand on two feet like a man; a human mind also was given to it. 5 And behold, another beast, a second one, resembling a bear. And it was raised up on one side, and three ribs [were] in its mouth between its teeth; and thus they said to it, 'Arise, devour much meat!'

This vision is reminiscent to that of Nebuchadnezzar's back in Daniel 2, which spoke of future kingdoms on the horizon. However, here in Daniel's vision, Daniel refers to these world powers as "beasts" not kingdoms. God will use the term "beast" again in the book of Revelation to give us insight into the methods and devices that the final beast kingdom is going to use to attempt to defeat Jesus Christ's people and His approaching rule.

The first beast in Daniel's vision corresponds with the head of gold in Nebuchadnezzar's dream, which we know to be Babylon. The image of the lion connotes pride and strength, and also speaks accurately of how

God humbled Nebuchadnezzar during his reign on earth by causing him to lose his sanity and live with the beasts of the field for seven years (Dan. 4:25). When Nebuchadnezzar came back to his senses he realized that the God in heaven is also the God who controls and determines who sits on the thrones in the earth.

The second beast, a bear, is looked on as the next strongest beast compared to a lion, and is known for its voracity but it lacks the speed and agility of the lion, all these being characteristics of the Medo-Persian Empire. The way the Medes conquered their enemies was by overwhelming them with the sheer mass of their armies which at times would run into the millions. The "three ribs" that are in the bear's mouth stand for the three kingdoms of Lydia, Babylon, and Egypt, which formed a "Triple Alliance" in order to protect themselves and hold the Medo-Persian power in check. Their efforts ultimately failed thus leading to their eventual demise.

> ***Daniel 7:6*** After this I kept looking, and behold, another one, like a leopard, which had on its back four wings of a bird; the beast also had four heads, and dominion was given to it.

This description of a third beast that was "like as a leopard" is an accurate reference to Alexander the Great in that the leopard symbolizes the quickness and military genius that Alexander used in conquering his enemies. This analogy of a leopard is also used in Revelation 13:2 when describing the quickness and military skill of the final beast empire. The four heads of this third beast are used to further define what happened to Alexander's kingdom after his early death; his empire was divided among his four generals which became the regions of Asia Minor, Syria, Egypt and Macedonia.

> ***Daniel 7:7*** After this I kept looking in the night visions, and behold, a fourth beast, dreadful and terrifying and extremely strong; and it had large iron teeth. It devoured and crushed, and trampled down the remainder with its feet; and it was different from all the beasts that were before it, and it had ten horns.

It is here in the vision of Daniel that we again see the characteristics of the fourth beast power. It says the Roman Empire would rule with an iron-fist and it would have dominion over the world. We know from history that this was certainly the case. It is also important to see that God, by way of Daniel's vision, gives us new information; that out of the Roman Empire would come ten "horns," a term used in the Bible for seats of power.

> ***Daniel 7:8*** While I was contemplating the horns, behold, another horn, *a little one,* came up among them, and three of the first horns were pulled out by the roots before it; and behold, this horn possessed eyes like the eyes of a man, and a mouth uttering great [boasts].

Out of these ten seats of power from the Roman Empire, a little power would arise that would be boastful and would subdue three of the ten horns in its quest for power. Verse 24 and 25 explain it further...

> ***Daniel 7:24*** As for the ten horns, out of this kingdom [Rome] ten kings will arise; and another will arise after them [the little horn], and he will be different from the previous ones and will subdue three kings. ***25*** And he will speak out against the Most High and wear down the saints of the Highest One, and he will intend to make alterations in times and in law; and they will be given into his hand for a time, times, and half a time. (italicized words added)

By carefully reading this section, we can see that out of the Roman Empire (the fourth beast) there will be ten horns, or countries. This is exactly what took place historically upon the demise of the Roman Empire. H. Grattan Guinness, author of *The Divine Program of the World's History* stated it this way:

> The historian Machiavelli, without the slightest reference to this prophecy, gives the following list of the nations which occupied the territory of the Western Empire at the time of the fall of Romulus Augustus (476 AD), the last emperor of Rome: the Lombards, the Franks, the Burgundians, the Ostrogoths, the Visigoths, the Vandals, the Heruli, the Suevi, the Huns, and the Saxons; ten in all.[1]

These ten countries comprise the area of what we know today as Spain, Germany, Switzerland, Portugal, Britain, France, and Italy. The Scripture tells that out of these ten regions would arise "a little horn," an infant country, that "shall be different from the previous ones" and the little horn shall subdue three kings. This little horn is going to speak *"great words against the most High, and shall wear out the saints of the most High, and think to change times and laws: and they shall be given into his hand until a time and times and the dividing of time."* (Dan. 7:25)

One can see direct similarities between Daniel's vision and Nebuchadnezzar's dream in regards to the four major kingdoms it speaks about, but we need to pay strict attention to the interpretation the angel gave Daniel of the vision.

> ***Daniel 7:16*** I approached one of those who were standing by and began asking him the exact meaning of all this. So he told me and made known to me the interpretation of these things: ***17*** 'These great beasts, which are four [in number,] are four kings [who] will arise from the earth. ***18*** But the saints of the Highest One will receive the kingdom and possess the kingdom forever, for all ages to come.' ***19*** Then I desired to know the exact meaning of the fourth beast, which was different from all the others, exceedingly dreadful, with its teeth of iron and its claws of bronze, [and which] devoured, crushed, and trampled down the remainder with its feet, ***20*** and [the meaning] of the ten horns that [were] on its head, and the other [horn] which came up, and before which three [of them] fell, namely, that horn which had eyes and a mouth uttering great [boasts,] and which was larger in appearance than its associates. ***21*** I kept looking, and that horn was waging war with the saints and overpowering them ***22*** until the Ancient of Days came, and judgment was passed in favor of the saints of the Highest One, and the time arrived when the saints took possession of the kingdom.

What is the passage saying? It is saying in verse 20 that out from the midst of the ten "horns," or seats of power left from the Roman Empire, there will come a new nation, diverse from all the rest that will speak great things, be arrogant and boastful, and will be larger in size than its "associates" when compared to the other horns. This little horn is going to "pluck out by the roots" three kings (from among the ten horns) and it will speak great words against the most High, and make war with the saints for 3½ years. After the 3½ years, Jesus Christ will return in glory, destroy the kingdoms of the world, and cause His kingdom to reign forever and ever.

These truths about the rise of the final beast are explicit and clear, but as we will see, they are going to be further elaborated on in Daniel chapters 9 and 12 and in Revelation, chapters 13, 17, and 18. When we get through studying these Scriptures, and put together the insights gained, it will bring us to the point that we can know with certainty who the "little horn" is that is going to bring about so much pain and hardship on God's people.

Before we go on and discover the details about this particular horn and its development into the final beast kingdom, let us review what Daniel 2 and Daniel 7 have shown us.

In Nebuchadnezzar's dream, God revealed that after Rome, another empire (the feet with ten toes) would arise that has both the strength of the Roman Empire as signified by iron, and would also be part clay, signifying the inclusion of weaker countries made up of various nationalities. This description of world government is made plainer still by the statement "they will combine with one another in the seed of men."

Daniel's vision then explains how the world government comes about. It says that out of the ten horns, or vestiges of the Roman Empire, will come a little horn which is *different* from all the others and it will "pluck out" three of the ten horns, and after doing so, it will rise in prominence and arrogance until it ultimately leads the one-world government that Christ will come and destroy. Look at the chart below to comprehend this truth.

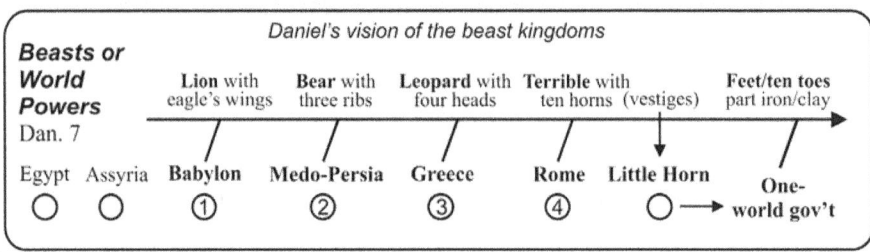

This chart shows the four kingdoms, Babylon, Medo-Persia, Greece, and the Roman Empire all lining up with each other in both historical order and characteristics. The fourth part of the statue which has legs of iron, and the fourth "terrifying" beast are without a doubt the same thing — the Roman Empire. The little horn then, coming out from within the ten horns has to be the world power we see before the final one-world government arrives because in Daniel 2 we see Rome, then the one-world government, then Christ's rule. Here in Daniel 7 we see Rome, the little horn rising to power and being destroyed by Jesus Christ, and then Christ's rule begins. Thus, the little horn has to be directly involved with the implementation of the final world government.

Having seen how all this fits, one needs to ask themselves the question, "What nation today fulfills the following criteria?"

1. What nation came out from the midst of the areas we now know to be Britain, Spain, France, Germany, Switzerland, Portugal, and Italy?
2. What nation is set apart and diverse from all these countries, yet has the military and economic might of the former Roman Empire?
3. What nation has proven to be larger in size than its "associates?" *(associates being the nations of Europe)*
4. What nation routed out or "subdued" three of the vestiges of the Roman Empire during its rise to power and prominence? *(Hint: use France, England, and Spain as vestiges)*
5. What nation boasts of itself as being the greatest nation on the face of the earth?

Answer: **The United States of America** is the only **nation** in the world that fits all the essential criteria of being the "little horn."

What about Russia being the "little horn" that leads the nations into one-world government? It cannot be because Daniel says the little horn came out from *within* the ten horns of Rome as a young emerging nation made up of Roman nationalities. Russia had been around for centuries prior to the Roman Empire and does not have the vast wealth and awe of the nations that the beast is spoken of having in the eighteenth chapter of book of Revelation. It cannot be China because of the ethnic considerations, and it cannot be Germany because it says the little horn was *diverse* from all the other horns and larger than its associates.

Of course you then have Rome, from which so many commentaries say the final beast or antichrist must emerge. Does the Scripture substantiate such a claim? No, for it says the little horn is *diverse* from those regions of the world, it is *larger* than any of the ten horns, and in addition, it will be in the habit of uttering great and prideful boasts. Are

Italy and the city of Rome boasting about being in the position to lead the nations into world government? Of course not, yet *the United States is, and continues to be the self-proclaimed economic and military superpower of the world.* In fact, that particular message continues to be drummed out each and every day by this nation in order to remind the countries around the globe that they ought to line up with the United States' democratic "ideals."

Given the evidence that the United States of America meets all the criteria to be the "little horn" spoken of in Daniel 7, we can now go to the book of Revelation and see how this "little horn" will propel and guide the rest of the nations of the world into a comprehensive, totalitarian world-government.

REVELATION 13

To begin looking into the book of Revelation, we need to first establish the source of the information we seek:

> ***Revelation 1:1*** The Revelation of Jesus Christ, which God gave unto him, to shew unto his servants things which must shortly come to pass; and he sent and signified [it] by his angel unto his servant John: *2* Who bare record of the word of God, and of the testimony of Jesus Christ, and of all things that he saw, *3* Blessed [is] he that readeth, and they that hear the words of this prophecy, and keep those things which are written therein: for the time [is] at hand. (KJV)

Scripture states plainly that the things revealed in the book of Revelation are from Christ Himself, and His purpose is to show us, His servants, what must shortly come to pass. This revelation, which God gave to Jesus Christ, was written down by the Apostle John and continues to build on the information given in the book of Daniel.

In the thirteenth chapter of Revelation, the Apostle John now labels world powers as "heads" and he uses the term "beast" to describe the world government system that the United States will ultimately lead the nations of the world into. The rise of this one-world government is described as follows:

> ***Revelation 13:1*** And he [John] stood on the sand of the seashore. And I saw a beast coming up out of the sea, having

ten horns and seven heads, and on his horns [were] ten diadems, and on his heads [were] blasphemous names.

In this vision, God gives us an all-encompassing view as to the breadth and source of the final beast's power. The seven heads represent the world's great powers that include their vast geographic domain, namely the Egyptians, the Assyrians, Babylonians, Medo-Persians, Greeks, and the Romans, with the United States being the seventh one as shown in the chart below.

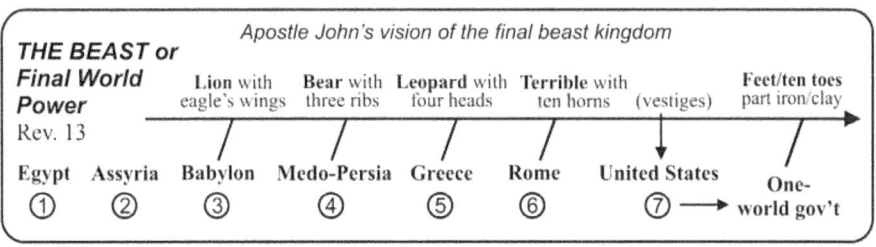

We see from the chart that both Egypt and Assyria, two world powers that affected Israel and controlled much of the world before Babylon, can be included in this vision because it is looking back on the history of man as a whole. In this context, the United States, the little horn, turns out to be the seventh beast, the forerunner of the final eighth beast power.

> ***Revelation 13:2*** And the beast which I saw was like a leopard, and his feet were like [those] of a bear, and his mouth like the mouth of a lion. And the dragon gave him his power and his throne and great authority.

The attributes given to this beast, like a leopard, feet as a bear, and mouth as a lion, all coincide with the former expressions God used to describe the strength, military might, and boldness under which the former world powers operated when controlling the world. It is very important to realize that the dragon, otherwise known as Satan, is spoken as the source of this world government's power, for it says that Satan gave this beast his throne, his power and great authority. These are the same rewards that the devil offered Jesus if only He would fall down and worship him (Matt. 4:8, 9). The infrastructure of leadership and much of big business in the United States has since taken Satan up on his bribe by selling its soul, its people, and the rest of the world to the god of materialism and self. If this seems ludicrous, merely look on where our government promotes dependence. It downplays God and the churches originally designed by God to take care of the needy, and instead promotes dependence on government, through the confiscation of citizen's money via the IRS that in turn feeds a bureaucracy instead of the people in need. Nearly 80% of the money designated for relief of the poor is eaten up in government overhead while organizations such as The Salvation Army, operating out of love and free will offerings, spends nearly 94% of its income in direct aid to those in need. Government finds a way to continually feed itself and the power structure within and it does so under the guise of helping the poor.

Big business, advertisers, and multi-national companies care little how deeply in debt the average wage earner becomes for their job is to make you want more so you will buy their product. It does not matter who wants to buy it either, as long as they get their money. Take for example the country of Red China. *The Guinness Book of World Records* lists Red China as history's most murderous government. The Senate Internal Security Subcommittee in 1971 estimated the casualties due to communism in China at between 34.3 and 63.8 million people. In March of 1956, *Time* magazine said the figures "stagger the imagination. In no previous war, revolution or human holocaust, or in the time of Hitler, have so many people been destroyed in so short a period." Even as I write, the government of China continues to practice genocide on young girls, leaving them to starve to death in "dying rooms." What is the United States' response? Our leaders give these murderers most favored nation (MFN) trade status! Is this what our country does to show concern for the poor?

In an April 24th *Washington Post* article, reporter Peter Behr reported that adopting voluntary codes of conduct for doing business in Communist China "...is a role U.S. business wants no part of according to corporate leaders and heads of business lobbying organizations." The article quotes the soon-to-be chairman of the National Association of Manufacturers as saying, "We would find that very onerous." The article goes on to say that most business leaders feel if US companies tried to pressure China on human rights they would soon be sent home, shut out of perhaps "the most fantastic economic opportunity in history." In light of this, does one have to wonder why 1 Timothy 6:10 says the LOVE of money is the root of all evil? Wretched communistic regimes would die a quick and natural death if not for the massive infusion of aid, food, and sophisticated technology that both our government and the military-industrial complex is more than happy to supply regardless of the human suffering such sales continue to inflict upon mankind. We go back to Revelation 13:3...

> ***Revelation 13:3*** And [I saw] one of his heads as if it had been slain, and his fatal wound was healed. And the whole earth was amazed [and followed] after the beast; ***4*** and they worshiped the dragon, because he gave his authority to the beast; and they worshiped the beast, saying, "Who is like the beast, and who is able to wage war with him?

Scripture tells us here that one of these seven "heads" had a wound as if it had been killed. Revelation 13:14 further describes this wound as having a "wound by a sword, and did live." It is at this point that most Christians stray off the path of logic and understanding by concluding that this mortal "head wound" is an actual wound inflicted upon an actual person namely "antichrist," who upon being slain, will be resurrected before the world and thus gain worship and allegiance. This conclusion cannot be true for Revelation 13:3 says of this beast, *"and I saw one of his heads as if it had been slain, and his fatal wound was healed."* If this wound was to a literal man, then this man also would have to have seven heads, feet like a bear, and a mouth like a lion, which is obviously not the case. The Apostle John here must be referring to world powers just as Daniel referred to world powers as beasts back in Daniel 7.

For those who want to persist with the idea of the antichrist being a literal man by citing the usage of the pronouns "he" and "his" throughout chapter 13, one needs to realize that the word "beast" is the Greek word *therion*, and it is neuter gender, neither masculine or feminine. This important truth is side-stepped in both the King James and the New International Version whereas some Bible translations, such as the Revised Standard Version, Phillips translation and the early Greek papyrus manuscripts translate this pronoun "it." This more accurate rendering of the pronoun further establishes the beast as a governmental power as described in the book of Daniel."[2]

"Antichrist," that word which conjures up images of a maniacal and demon-possessed leader needs to be more closely looked at also since it is used only five times in the Bible and in fact does not even appear in the book of Revelation! The way the word "antichrist" is used in its context is very enlightening.

> *1 John 2:18* Children, it is the last hour; and just as you heard that antichrist is coming, even now many antichrists have arisen; from this we know that it is the last hour.
>
> *1 John 2:22* Who is the liar but the one who denies that Jesus is the Christ? This is the antichrist, the one who denies the Father and the Son.
>
> *1 John 4:1* Beloved, do not believe every spirit, but test the spirits to see whether they are from God; because many false prophets have gone out into the world. *2* By this you know the Spirit of God: every spirit that confesses that Jesus Christ has come in the flesh is from God; *3* and every spirit that does not confess Jesus is not from God; and this is the [spirit] of the antichrist, of which you have heard that it is coming, and now it is already in the world.
>
> *2 John 7* For many deceivers have gone out into the world, those who do not acknowledge Jesus Christ [as] coming in the flesh. This is the deceiver and the antichrist.

According to the Scriptures just cited, "antichrist" is anyone who denies Jesus Christ and intends to deceive others of the same.

As the United States and the rest of the world fall deeper and deeper into sin and apostasy towards the truth as mentioned in 2 Timothy 3:1-5; it will give rise to an all pervasive spirit of hatred and rebellion against the truth and the authority of God. This attitude will truly bring about a time of "antichrist," which means according to Strong's Concordance, "adversary of the Messiah."

If we consider we are now talking about a world power in Revelation 13:3 as opposed to a person, then this near fatal wound by a "sword" would suggest a military defeat so devastating that it was looked on as miraculous that the nation survived. Not only that, but Scripture tells us that it will be through this miraculous recovery from military defeat that both the beast and Satan become an object of worship to the world because of the beast's invincible strength. This truth is made evident by what we see the inhabitants of the earth saying at this particular time:

Revelation 13:4(b) and they *[the inhabitants]* worshiped the beast, saying, 'Who is like the beast, and who is able to wage war with him?'

The Wound by a Sword

We have seen that all indicators point to the United States being the seventh world power according to the chronology of world powers revealed in Daniel 7. Now one needs to ask themselves the question in regard to verse 4 and one of the "heads" being wounded, "What military wound did the United States experience as a nation that caused it to become the world's largest economic and military power? The answer is *the bombing of Pearl Harbor,* that "day of infamy" as Roosevelt called it, when in less than an hour the United States experienced a massive hemorrhage of its military strength. Where at one moment you had 353 planes on the airstrips poised and ready for action, minutes later 341 of those planes were either damaged or destroyed. Where 146 United States warships floated in the waters of Pearl Harbor during early dawn, minutes later over 19 ships including eight battleships were left sunk or heavily damaged. The *USS Arizona* alone took 1,177 young men down to its watery grave. This attack on Pearl Harbor was planned a full year in advance by the Commander of the Japanese Naval Forces, and was carried out in his own words, to "mortally wound" the military capabilities of the United States.[3] The Japanese however never conceived that through this "mortal wound," the United States government and the American people would rally to the point that they would become the most awesome and revered nation on the face of the earth. Yet that is exactly what has happened.

Ever since it's decisive victory in World War II and its entrance into the United Nations, the United States has been slowly and methodically moving toward bringing all nations in under a global government with the United Nations being the cover. To convince you of this truth is not the purpose of this book nor is it available within the scope of this study. Let it be said however, that in my opinion the United States is not the *sole* purveyor of this globalist dream, but will be consummated through a multi-faceted linkage of global idealists in both the free world *and* communistic countries. The key to understand is that the United States is the mother of them all, for it is from this country and its channels of money that both communist and socialist nations have continued to be fed. Let it also be known that it is from New York City, haven for both industrialists and one-world ideologues, that many of these important decisions are made — not Washington.

Listen to what Paul H. Nitze, veteran member of the Council on Foreign Relations had to say in a speech celebrating the opening of a new Council on Foreign Relations office in Washington. After taking the time to describe the Council's influence during the 1920's and 1930's, he said:

> The State Department and White House might conduct diplomacy in peace and raise and command armies in war, but policy was made by serious people, men with a longer view, i.e. the great men of finance and their advisers. New York was where they were to be found.

He went on to say about his organization:

> In the postwar years, the Council has continued to represent an invaluable way for many of us Washingtonians to tap the enormously important New York business and intellectual community.[4]

This influence of the New York City elite should not be underestimated, nor the influential power brokers through which their goals are communicated. H. Rowan Gaither, a CFR member and past president of the well-known and extremely powerful Ford Foundation made a frank admission to Norman Dodd, the director of research for the congressional committee investigating the activities of tax-exempt foundations in 1953. In a private meeting to discuss why Congress wanted to investigate the foundations, Rowan Gaither told Dodd that for years he and others had worked for the State Department, the United Nations, and other Federal agencies during which time he and others

> . ..operated under directives issued by the White House, the substance of which was that we should make every effort to so alter life in the United States as to make possible a comfortable merger with the Soviet Union.[5]

As an afterthought, Rowan then said, "We are continuing to be guided by just such directives." When the flabbergasted Dodd asked Gaither if he would repeat the statement to the full House Committee, Gaither replied, "This we would not think of doing." The sad truth is that

The Origin and Identity of the Beast

the goal of many of our government leaders is to make the United States into a socialist state, and then merge all nations into a one-world government controlled by a powerful few. Is this hard for you to believe or imagine? Then just read the ten planks of Marx and Engel's famed *Communist Manifesto* and see if we are unknowingly on the brink of being a confirmed socialist state.

1. <u>Abolition of property in land and application of all rents of land to public purposes.</u> *(Ask anyone in the Southwest or Northwest these days if this is not happening to them as the government takes over private land under the auspices of the Endangered Species Act or Federal Wetlands Act.)*

2. <u>A heavy progressive or graduated income tax.</u> *(Our burdensome tax system has continued to be a key campaign issue for the last two decades.)*

3. <u>Abolition of all right of inheritance.</u> *(To those who have experienced it, the present inheritance tax amounts to sheer theft from the families the departed loved one sought to provide for.)*

4. <u>Confiscation of the property of all emigrants and rebels.</u> *(Thanks to the Comprehensive Forfeiture Act of 1984, both rebels and innocent citizens are having their assets, their homes, and their cars confiscated by law enforcement officials on the mere suspicion of being involved with illegal drugs.)*[6]

5. <u>Centralization of credit in the hands of the state, by means of a national bank with state capital and an exclusive monopoly.</u> *(The Federal Reserve anyone?)*

6. <u>Centralization of the means of communication and transport in the hands of the state.</u> *(TV and radio stations cannot operate unless under the watchful eye of the Federal Communications Commission, nor can transport companies operate unless they meet all the stringent requirements of the Department of Transportation).*

7. <u>Extension of factories and instruments of production owned by the state; the bringing into cultivation of waste lands, and the improvement of the soil generally in accordance with a common plan.</u> *(The EPA, Soil Conservation Service, and the Bureau of Land Management fit this description nicely, especially if you have tried to comply with their demands.)*

8. <u>Equal liability of all to labor. Establishment of industrial armies,</u>

especially for agriculture. *(This transformation will take place when government moves even further into people's lives when crisis hits this country.)*

9. Combination of agriculture with manufacturing industries; gradual abolition of the distinction between town and country by a more equable distribution of population over the country. *(Yet to be realized, but as can be seen from the FEMA laws in place for times of "national emergency," this type of redistribution of individuals to locations designated by government can take place.)*

10. Free education for all children in public schools. Abolition of children's factory labour in its present form. Combination of education with industrial production.[7] *(Government job training, public schools, and labor laws are all deeply imbedded within our culture.)*

Karl Marx would be proud we've come such a long way towards attaining the model attributes of a purely socialistic state, yet people in this country are barely waking up to how far our nation has fallen from the God-given rights afforded us by the Constitution. With these things in mind concerning the rise of the seventh beast, we can see according to Revelation 17:3 and verse 7 that the United States will lead all other nations into world government.

> ***Revelation 17:3*** And he carried me away in the Spirit into a wilderness; and I saw a woman sitting on a scarlet beast, full of blasphemous names, having seven heads and ten horns. **7** And the angel said to me, "Why do you wonder? I shall tell you the mystery of the woman and of the beast that carries her, which has the seven heads and the ten horns.

The beast that has the seven heads and ten horns that we first saw in Revelation 13:1 will now be explained for us by the angel:

> ***Revelation 17:9*** Here is the mind which has wisdom. The seven heads are seven mountains on which the woman sits, and they are seven kings; five have fallen, one is, the other has not yet come; and when he comes, he must remain a little while.

In this Scripture, God unveils human history both past and future. The seven heads are seven mountains that represent the geographical area

The Origin and Identity of the Beast

that fell under the control of these heads. It says the seven heads are also seven kings which have had power and authority over the earth. Look at the chart below to better understand these truths. It will be helpful to follow along with the chart as you read Revelation 17:9-11.

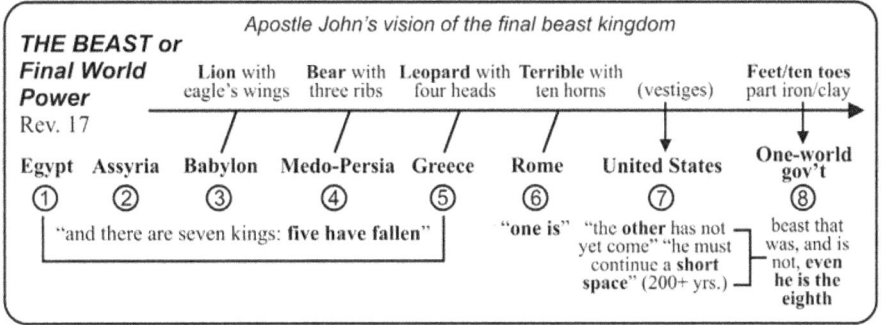

Revelation 17:9 Here is the mind which has wisdom. The seven heads are seven mountains on which the woman sits, and they are seven kings; **five have fallen, one is, the other has not yet come; and when he comes, he must remain a little while.** *11* And the beast which was and is not, is himself also an eighth, and is [one] of the seven, and he goes to destruction. (emphasis added)

We can now understand God's total view of mankind's history. The Apostle John was told in regards to world powers, that five had fallen, which were the kingdoms of Egypt, Assyria, Babylon, Medo-Persia, and Greece. He was then told "one is," which would correspond to the Roman Empire which was still in power at the time John wrote the book of Revelation. The next nation is referred to as "the other has not yet come," because it had not yet appeared on the world scene, but John was told that "when he comes, he must remain a little while." This statement perfectly describes the United States of America. It was born from the nationalities of the fallen Roman Empire and upon arriving; it only remains "a little while." The United States is just over two hundred years old, making it a mere infant compared to the thousands of years other countries and nationalities of the world have been in existence. The accuracy of God's Word is astounding!

> **Revelation 17:11** And the beast which was and is not, is himself also an eighth, and is [one] of the seven, and he goes to destruction.

The United States, which according to Scripture is only to remain "a little while," will be transformed into the eighth and final beast empire. We can know this by reading Revelation 17:11 carefully.

> **And the beast which was** *[the United States]* **and is not,** *[there is a time coming when it will no longer be the United States]* **is himself also an eighth,** *[when it is transformed from the seventh into the eighth]* **and is [one] of the seven,** *[right now the US is the mystery seventh beast]* **and he goes to destruction,** *[when it is destroyed by Jesus Christ as part of the final beast system]* (italicized words added)

From reading Revelation 13 and 17 we are told that the final eighth beast empire, the New World Order, will arise and be led into power by the United States of America. It is going to be a totalitarian, one-world government that will have power over "all kindred, tongues and nations." How will such a world-wide government be managed? Revelation 17:12-13 provides us the answer.

> **Revelation 17:12** And the ten horns which you saw are ten kings, who have not yet received a kingdom, but they receive authority as kings with the beast for one hour. **13** These have one purpose and they give their power and authority to the beast.

This verse can be understood in light of the plans already set down by the globalist elite. The Club of Rome (COR), a think-tank organization comprised of scientists, educators, economists, humanists, industrialists, and other national and international civil servants, was commissioned by the insider elite to prepare a report for the regionalization and unification of the entire world. On September 17, 1973 they published their report called *Regionalized and Adaptive Model of the Global World System*. In the report they divided the world into ten "kingdoms". When the call for global unification finally arrives, which will most likely be due to world-wide economic and social chaos stemming from the birth pangs of God's judgment beginning to erupt on earth, these ten magna-regions could very well be the vehicle whereby world government is established. According to Revelation 17:12-13, the rulers who preside over these "kingdoms" will be given authority with the beast for a very short time. Why only a short time? Because the final beast kingdom only has power for 3½ years to exert its power as declared in the book of Daniel. These regions then, correspond to the "ten toes" of the statue in Nebuchadnezzar's dream, the statue whose feet portrayed a one-world government that Jesus Christ would ultimately come to destroy.

Excerpt from **Club of Rome Report**: *Regionalized and Adaptive Model of the Global World System; Strategy For Survival Project* (Behold a Pale Horse, by William Cooper, 1991 pg. 456; Light Technology Publishing, Sedona, AZ)

We have seen that the United States of America fulfills in a dynamic way the criteria needed to indeed be the seventh beast, the world power which the book of Revelation says will arise before the end. It is now necessary to go further into the Word of God and see exactly how the final eighth beast system gains control over the world and what every Christian needs to be aware of in these the last days.

REVELATION UNRAVELED

Chapter 2

The Mark of the Beast

Having now discovered who the beast is in the book of Revelation, let us now direct our attention to how the beast will be able to successfully implement a one-world government and keep vast areas of the world under its control.

The methodology that the beast will employ is set forth in Revelation chapter 13 starting in verse 11:

> ***Revelation 13:11*** And I beheld another beast coming up out of the earth; and he had two horns like a lamb, and he spake as a dragon.

From what the Apostle John describes about the final beast kingdom in verses one through ten, we know that the beast will have dominion over the saints for 3½ years, and that much persecution will take place. Verse eleven tells us one of the sources of control the final beast will use during this time. It says *another beast* will arise out of the earth, and this beast will have two horns like a lamb, but it will speak like a dragon.

In past records, we have seen that "horns" symbolize power, and here the analogy is the same. We can be sure this beast is to be understood figuratively because a lamb, which is in reality a young sheep and less than one year old, does not have horns. This beast also appears harmless like a lamb, yet speaks *like a dragon,* certainly something sheep do not do. What then do these things mean?

To address this question, I recommend the book, *Last Days in America* by Bob Fraley.[8] In his book, Mr. Fraley gives a powerful testimony of how God gave his brother Charles, a vivid revelation about the meaning of this particular beast, and it was the power of this insight along with another about the identity of the final beast kingdom, that caused Charles to carry out his commitment to God to be a medical missionary in Africa. This divine insight also caused Bob Fraley's life to be changed in that he felt moved by God to devote much of his time and energy over the years to both research and write on how the two revelations fit with the Word of God.

I have read and exposed myself to much of what is on bookshelves today in the area of Bible prophecy and what authors claim certain things mean in the book of Revelation. I truly believe that the insight God gave to Charles Fraley to explain just one small facet of the Word, provides every student of the Bible a perspective about the devil's method of operation that is sorely needed in these last days.

We read in verse twelve that this "other beast" that rises up is going to augment and enhance the rise to power of the United States to the point that "it causeth the earth and them which dwell therein to worship the first beast (the United States), whose deadly wound was healed."

What is the power that enables this to take place? Fraley says it is ***the power of electricity,*** and all the technology that it employs. Fraley saw the two horns of the gentle lamb signify the positive and negative charges of electricity, which when used by Satan for his purposes, speak as a dragon. What are Satan's purposes? One of his purposes is to use electricity's power to help drown the world in his lies and entrapments. What are some of the lies? One lie is that the United States is *the* great world power capable of bringing peace and justice to the world. That position of authority is reserved for one man and one man only — Jesus Christ. If Satan can successfully deceive people into thinking that men have the answers to the world's problems, then he has succeeded in drawing people away from the one true God. The word "worship" in verse 12 is the Greek word *proskuneo* and means "to pay homage to, to express respect or to make supplication." This attitude of "worship" I believe was evident at the signing of the armistice by the Japanese with the United States at the end of World War II, for only days earlier the whole world witnessed the massive power the United States unleashed via the technology of the atomic bomb. It was during that solemn ceremony which occurred on the *USS Missouri* that began I believe, the process of all the world "worshipping" the beast, the United States of America.

> ***Revelation 13:13*** And he doeth great wonders, so that he maketh fire come down from heaven on the earth in the sight of men. (KJV)

Whether this verse is a direct reference to the bombing of Hiroshima and Nagasaki that brought about the birth of the beast, or whether it is merely making reference to the power of electricity itself, I do not know. But it is interesting to note that electricity was called "fire from heaven" by its discoverer Benjamin Franklin. The Bible goes on to say in verse 14:

> **Revelation 13:14**... it deceiveth them that dwell on the earth by [the means of] those miracles which he had power to do in the sight of the beast; saying to them that dwell on the earth, that they should make an image to the beast, which had the wound by a sword, and did live.

Today the power of electricity is being used to deceive people on the earth. It is causing them to "worship" the beast that had the "wound by a sword and did live," which we know to be the United States. The ushering in of the New World Order will take place due to the "miracles" the second beast, electricity, is able to perform in the presence of the beast. What are the miracles John is making reference to? Virtually everything he saw in his vision that the power of electricity makes possible. Think about it. The Apostle John, living back in the time of the Roman Empire, is allowed to see by revelation the wonders of our modern day technology. It is no wonder he would say that this beast could do miracles for even today we use the term "miracle of technology" to describe all the amazing things man is able to accomplish and bring about through electricity's power!

But how is electricity being used to "speak as a dragon?" All you need to do is look in any bookstore, movie theater, or watch any television program and you will see a plethora of examples. Electricity is providing the *means* where ideas are moved en masse to people and those ideas promulgate the god of this world by encouraging everyone to be caught up into "the course of this world" which is based primarily on *"the lusts of the flesh, the lust of the eyes and the pride of life,"* all attitudes which 1 John 2:16 says, *"is not of the Father but is of the world."* America has been sold this ideology by Satan himself, and has been busy selling it to the rest of the world through the media and the advertising world ever since the end of World War II. Before this time, America had what historians would regard as firm roots in the Judeo-Christian work ethic and biblical principles. But as years have gone by, our country has been indoctrinated with a steady diet of "doctrines of devils" and catering to the flesh, which as a result has caused our society and the rest of the world to plummet both morally and spiritually. All this because we have turned away from the truth of God's Word in our pulpits and have succumbed to the slow and steady lie that to have more is always better. We have been tricked as a society into believing that the principles which God set up in His Word are no longer valid but should be thrown away and traded in for *new* behavior, behavior that would have been called perverse only a few years ago. The goal behind Satan's scheme is to get people to compromise, get used to it, compromise again, get used to it and before long, a person has no godly principles left! This is the methodology that has been at work in our culture for years. By way of technology, we have been drawn into the traps of Satan. The lusts of the flesh are fed through the advertising and the entertainment industry, while the pride of life is encouraged and stoked to the point that man basically puts himself on a pedestal and sees himself in control of his own destiny instead of humbling himself under the mighty hand of God who created him.

Ever since the end of World War II, our spiritual adversary has been using the wealth of the United States to steadily chip away at the biblical principles that used to be the American way of life. Listen to what President Teddy Roosevelt said back in his day:

> Americanism means the virtues of courage, honor, justice, truth, sincerity, and hardihood — the virtues that made America. The things that will destroy America are prosperity at any price, peace at any price, safety first instead of duty first, the love of soft living, and the get-rich-quick theory of life.

As a country we now have many of the attitudes that Teddy Roosevelt spoke against. Another deleterious effect that comes from our lifestyle of money and wealth is that Americans spend less time with their children than any other people on the face of the earth. This shift in priorities when it comes to nurturing our children is bound to have consequences on future generations, regardless of what modem psychologists say. Statistics already show that the decay of the family unit is well underway. The moral decline we are experiencing as a nation is really no different than what happened to the Roman Empire centuries ago. Jim Nelson Black mentions some of the parallels in his book, *When Nations Die*. He quotes the Roman poet Livy as saying,

Greed and self-indulgence led the Romans into dangerous excess. All this was set off by absorption with the vice of luxury. 'For it is true,' said Livy, 'that when men had fewer possessions, they were also modest in their desires. Lately riches have brought avarice and abundant pleasures, and the desire to carry luxury and lust to the point of ruin and universal perdition.' [9]

Another interesting statistic that speaks of our ever-increasing obsession with "things" is that at the end of World War II there were only eight shopping centers in the United States. Between 1970 - 1990 there were 25,000 more.

Spend some time in the ancient city of Carthage which at one time had enormous wealth, and you would see thousands of coffins lined up, row upon row of infants who were murdered and burned as sacrifices to their pagan goddess. Right now, the abortion rate in the United States stands at *1.6 million per year.* Black makes the point in his book that with over 30 million innocent children purposely killed in their mother's wombs over the last twenty years through the carnage of abortion, is America really any different than the pagans in Carthage? All that is different he says, is that we have instead sacrificed them on the altar of greed and materialism. [10]

Media-moguls and top business leaders of the world work feverishly and spend thousands of dollars in order to replace the biblical principles of stewardship. They counter the positive attribute of contentment with the time-worn notion that by accumulating more and more possessions you will be happy. The Bible clearly teaches that this is the wrong way to live. Look at what Jesus said in Luke 12:15.

> ***Luke 12:15*** And he said unto them, Take heed, and beware of covetousness: for a man's life consisteth not in the abundance of the things which he possesseth. (KJV)

Why does Jesus Christ say this? Because he knows where it can lead...

> ***1 Timothy 6:9*** But they that will be rich fall into temptation and a snare, and [into] many foolish and hurtful lusts, which drown men in destruction and perdition. (KJV)

Look at verse 17...

> ***1 Timothy 6:17*** Charge them that are rich in this world, that they be not high-minded, nor trust in uncertain riches, but in the living God, who giveth us richly all things to enjoy. (KJV)

Riches can be a dangerous and seductive tool of the adversary because it provides an open door for an individual to begin to trust oneself or one's money instead of trusting God. Jesus made this very clear in the Gospel of Luke, chapter 8 verse 14...

> ***Luke 8:14*** And that which fell among thorns are they, which, when they have heard, go forth, and are choked with cares and riches and pleasures of [this] life, and bring no fruit to perfection. (KJV)

Satan is a master at seducing man and causing him to turn away from God. He does this by building in man an inordinate lust for other things — a characteristic called covetousness in the Bible. Satan's whole battle plan has been perfectly played out by using his agents of darkness to promote the philosophy that it is perfectly acceptable to live beyond one's means. It is a lie from hell that has brought disastrous consequences.

For example, in the 1940's before the war ended, *saving* money was looked on as a sign of character. People seldom thought about buying such things as cars or appliances on credit, but instead opted to buy what they could afford and pay for them in cash. With the rise of the beast at the end of the World War II however, government expanded, entitlements were instituted, and credit began to take off so people could build the homes and buy the cars everyone felt *they deserved.* This was the foothold Satan wanted. As more people enjoyed having things and paying for it later, the debt level of most families continued to escalate; to the point that we have now reached a disastrous level of debt causing dangerous stresses on families, marriages, and society itself. At what cost do you think we enjoy the supposed "good life" that Satan has talked us into wanting? In the 1960's the average family (which at that time usually had only one wage earner) paid just 7% of their income in taxes and 15% of their income was spent on debt, primarily mortgages. Now in the 1990's, it takes *40% of two incomes* to pay all the debts that the average family has heaped upon themselves.

So what is Satan's next move? He is going to enslave man by way of his own greed, and Satan will do it with what is called the mark of the beast. In Revelation 13, God enlightens us as to how the coming one-world government will bring people under its control.

> ***Revelation 13:15*** And he *[2nd beast]* had power to give life unto the image of the beast *[the final beast system]*, that the image of the beast should both speak, and cause that as many as would not worship the image of the beast should be killed. (KJV) (italicized words added)

The word "life" in verse 15 is the word *pneuma,* which means spirit. It is interesting to know that this is the only instance where the word *pneuma* is translated "life." The Apostle John did not know what gave this image "life," so it could be he used the word "spirit" to convey the point that it was some invisible force that energized the image, just as the spirit moves us. Could it be that John was trying to describe electricity's power in a way he could understand? This force appeared to give life to the image of the beast. What is an image? An image is a likeness, a representation of something. So it is with the image of the beast, it will be a representation of the control and domination this one-world government will be exerting over the world.

> ***Revelation 13:15*** And he *[2nd beast, electricity]* had power to give life unto the image of the beast, that the image of the beast should both speak, and cause that as many as would not worship *[pay homage to]* the image of the beast should be killed. ***16*** And he causeth all, both small and great, rich and poor, free and bond, to receive a mark in their right hand, or in their foreheads: ***17*** And that no man might buy or sell, save he that had the mark, or the name of the beast, or the number of his name. (KJV) (italicized words added)

The next verse gives us a vital key in unlocking the mystery to the image of the beast.

> ***Revelation 13:18*** Here is wisdom. Let him that hath understanding count the number of the beast: for it is the number of a man; and his number [is] Six hundred threescore [and] six. (KJV)

REVELATION UNRAVELED

Over the decades man has continued to develop and build more and more sophisticated gadgets so he can have more and more creature comforts as he gains dominion over the earth. In order to help deal with the complexity of the affairs he has created for himself, man recently developed his crowning achievement — the computer. Man developed the computer to make his life easier — to do troublesome, tedious work and to provide the user with an efficient way to handle the volumes of information he or she learns and processes. In perhaps what will be the ultimate irony, Satan in the near future will use the computer, the brainchild of man's intellect, to bring all of mankind into slavery.

> ***Revelation 13:15*** And he had power to give life unto the image of the beast, that the image of the beast should both speak, and cause that as many as would not worship the image of the beast should be killed. ***16*** And he causeth all, both small and great, rich and poor, free and bond, to receive a mark in their right hand, or in their foreheads: ***17*** And that no man might buy or sell, save he that had the mark, or the name of the beast, or the number of his name. (KJV)

Satan's whole plan and how it is going to be implemented is already in place in that man has succeeded in getting virtually all facets of society to be tied into the computer, generated by that all powerful tool — electricity. Satan has lulled Christians to sleep concerning the dangers of this situation by keeping them wrapped up with the cares and worries of this world. With this all encompassing computer network stealthily in place, and by working within key men in government and business, Satan is going to enact a method of control that will assure compliance by nearly every person in the world, because it will be based on their desire for the things of this world. The form of control is called ***the mark of the beast*** and it is founded upon the UPC - the Universal Product Code. Do you know what this code is? It is the bar code that we see on everything we buy, and in this bar code we can see exactly what the Bible was talking about in Revelation 13:16-17.

The UPC Product Code

The Universal Product Code was devised to standardize an identification system whereby food — and all aspects of it, such as the manufacturer, size and flavor of the item, price, taxability etc. could be stored on computer. This identification system has been successful enough around the world that it is used on most every product bought or sold today. The way the system works is this. The bar code is made up of *marks* and these marks represent allocated numbers. In the Appendix of this book, you will see some examples of bar codes and how they are set up. The bar code at the top of page 174 shows that each mark within the code has varying widths and configurations and each particular mark corresponds to a number, the numbers being located at the bottom of the code. All the marks are identified except for three marks — one to the far left, one in the middle, and another on the far right side. The next bar code shows what the three unidentified marks would look like if they were isolated. The next figure down shows that the width and configuration of the three marks match up perfectly with the mark that corresponds to the number six, so you end up with three unidentified marks that correspond to 6, 6, 6. This configuration occurs on every bar code. Every bar code has three unidentified marks that one way or another always contain the numbers 6,6,6.

Why is the number 6 used so often? I would like to quote the reason from Bob Fraley's book, *Last Days in America.*

> The reason is that computers work on a series of 6 cores like the supermarket Model 304 produced by National Cash Register. It allows changing direction of current to performing switching operations. The 6 cores work in conjunction with 60 displacements X 6 - one character - one bit of information. The formula for this system is 6 60 6. To number a card, person or item, the transaction must be prefixed "six hundred, threescore and six." [11]

When one realizes that the Apostle John was accurately told by revelation some 2000 years ago that the world will be brought under economic control through a marking system based on 666, there is only one credible conclusion, and that is *the technology of the mark of the beast is here.*

If this UPC bar code system is already being used to identify every article being bought or sold around the nation and the world, could not this same system be used on people when the government demands that every individual be identified, as with a national identity card? Did you know that the magnetic strips on the back of credit cards and bank cards already have bar codes encoded on them and they are all pre-fixed with the number 666? Up to 100,000 characters can be micro-encoded on the strip, enough data to provide reams of information about you or your family to those who want to know.

So how is this powerful tool going to be used by Satan when he becomes fully manifest and empowers the final beast system in the last days? First, there is going to be a continued push for a *cashless economy* not only from the government but from the banking community as well. The benefit of the computer's data and storage capability is going to be used as the vehicle for this dangerous transformation as the stage gets set for worldwide economic control and slavery. As this electronic economy gets closer at hand, you will begin to see the birth pangs of God's judgment spoken about in Matthew 24, increasing and becoming more evident. Ecological and social catastrophes, discussed in chapters four and five, will be throwing the world into spiritual and economic chaos.

The coming economic crisis is going to be blamed on the runaway spending of our government and will affect not only the United States, but the tremors are going to be felt around the globe. When the economic earthquake takes place, governments around the world will step in with a plan to supposedly bring order. Part of that plan will be some sort of National Identity Card, or as is already being used on animals, an implantable bio-chip that will carry all the information the government deems necessary about you. The argument for it will be that it is theft-proof and counterfeit proof. If all this doesn't sound feasible to you, think again.

Implantable bio-chips are already being used throughout Europe and Canada to identify pets and keep accurate records of the livestock industry. The practice is now spreading in the United States where in fact Colorado Springs and dozens of other cities across America are replacing dog tags with bio-chips. When animals are picked up by the dog-catcher, they use a wand-like scanner, just like scanning a price on an item at the supermarket, in order to identify the owner of the pet. We can see this evidenced by an article in the *Oceanside Blade Citizen,* Sept. 18, 1993.

> Hector Cazares, acting director of the county Animal Control Department, said Friday that all pets adopted from the shelters... will be entered into an electronic identification system. A microchip transponder the size of a rice grain is injected under the pet's skin, usually behind the nape of the neck. An electronic scanner picks up the microchip's signal,

which transmits an identification number used to look up the *pet's name, owner, birth date, medical records and other details contained in a computer database.*

Right now these chips in the transponders have 35 "bits" of information in them which give them the possibility of issuing up to 34 billion different ID numbers, certainly enough to cover the population of the earth. Yet even this technology is being constantly upgraded.

Identification Devices, Inc., one of the leaders in the field of identification technology, recently wrote in one of their promotional flyers where they believe this technology is likely to go in the future...[12]

> Suppose you were to make a list of the technical advances that are quickly reshaping the way we live: micro-miniaturization of electronic components, high speed data processing systems, powerful new computer programming techniques and extremely sophisticated telecommunication devices... *Then consider how these innovations might be employed to solve the age old problem of providing positive identification of people,* animals and equipment. (emphasis added)

How does this tie in with Satan's plans? When the one-world government comes on the scene, the technology already in place and already proven will be used to implement a world-wide identification system. At this stage I believe the "image of the beast" will be the electronic scanner that will be in every store around the world in order to read the UPC code off the product you buy, and electronically credit the number or code from the bio-chip implant placed either in the right hand or the forehead of the purchaser. Only time will tell exactly how it will all work out, but what is critical to understand is that when this system is implemented in its fullness, it will most likely involve some sort of agreement or coercion on the part of every individual taking the implant. I believe that in order for you to receive the implant and operate within the new cashless society, you will have to pledge your allegiance to the all powerful state, and deny your Christian faith. *Monetary control* will be the means whereby true Christians in the New World Order will be identified and snuffed out, for dedicated followers of Christ are the number one enemy of any totalitarian state in that they are compelled to obey God rather than men. For those individuals whose Christian faith means little to them, they will gladly renounce their faith in order to "gain their mess of pottage." Because of their ignorance of spiritual matters, due in part to what little Bible has been taught in church pulpits, they will not even realize they are selling their birthright to the kingdom of God, but indeed they will be, *because the Bible says anyone who takes the mark of the beast will be damned.* Satan is a master manipulator and yet how ignorant man has also allowed himself to become.

    This critical test of allegiance has been asked many times in years past by Christians outside of the United States whose countries have been taken over by repressive Communist regimes. Many wonderful saints have bravely given up what little they did own in worldly goods, even to the point of forfeiting their lives, rather than denying the One they knew and loved, Jesus Christ. This incredible stand for truth will not take place in America when the crisis hits however, because many churches in this country are filled with people who look on Christianity merely as an acceptable social duty, just another lifestyle to identify with. There is no real love for Christ within these people; they are merely in church to be entertained and to be seen, their social responsibilities met. But watch, when the storm clouds of unrest and judgment begin to descend upon this country, the lifestyle that many Americans have come to expect is going to disappear and then the real, honest soul-searching will begin. Those who have their lifestyle built on debt are going to see their financial dreams wiped out and there will be pain, anguish, and fear upon every American who does not rest their hope in Almighty God. During that time of fear and uncertainty people are going to be hard pressed to make up for all the lost time they spent in unbelief and selfish living. God will come to judge and try men's souls. Are you one of those individuals? If so, repent, come to God and get close to the Lord Jesus Christ — NOW!

    Every American and those living in other countries are going to have to make a decision when the mark of the beast identification system comes to pass at the hand of world government. You will be forced to ask yourself, "Do I want to continue to function within the economic system of the world and keep much of what I have by willingly renouncing the things the government tells me to renounce, or am I going to stand for Christ and the Word of God and be left as an outcast, not being able to buy or sell because I fail to accept the mark of the beast?" That will be the question and the issue for which God will hold people responsible. For those of you who want to be among the elect who will never be asked to face that decision, I encourage you to study the rest of this book carefully for Jesus Christ does give us guidance, so that in His words, *"you may be accounted worthy to escape all these things that shall come to pass, and to stand before the Son of man."* (Luke 21:36)

REVELATION UNRAVELED

Chapter 3

The Seventy Weeks of Daniel

When it comes to understanding "the end times" or what many call "the last days," it is imperative that we understand a subject of Scripture considered to be the bedrock of prophecy — the Seventieth Week of Daniel. If you can understand this topic, the book of Revelation and the whole scenario of the end times will make sense like never before.

We have gone into the book of Daniel and gained some tremendous insight into identifying the "little horn," the seventh head of the final beast system that is described in Revelation 13. This seventh head, which I believe to be the United States of America, is going to be the *prime mover* of bringing the nations of the world together under the rule of one-world government. This transformation will most likely be accomplished by the introduction of UN forces within the cities of the world as a means to bring calm and control to the havoc that will ensue as the seals spoken of in the book of Revelation begin to take their effect on earth.

The timing of these "seals" can be both understood and expected as we go further into our study of both the book of Daniel and the book of Revelation. God gives us the information as to who, when, how and why these judgments are coming to pass on the earth so we as Christians are not left ignorant or spiritually unprepared.

Before we go on and study these impending judgments, I would like to cover some important principles first.

1. We need to understand that God is omnipotent and that He has a plan for the nations, even the wicked. Proverbs 16:4 says *"The LORD has made everything for its own purpose, even the wicked for the day of evil."* Neither you nor I may totally understand this verse, but regardless of how we feel, we need to accept how God plans to deal with mankind.

2. Once the event takes place that signals the beginning of the Seventieth Week of Daniel, there is no turning back from God's timetable. The last seven years of human history will have begun.

REVELATION UNRAVELED

Daniel's Prayer

Chapter nine of the book of Daniel describes a scene in which the prophet receives one of the most important revelations in the Bible. Verses 3-19 tell us how Daniel was deep in prayer and supplication before the Lord, confessing the sins of the people of Israel; asking God to forgive them for rejecting His laws. Daniel pleaded for mercy on the people who were scattered about and for God to once again restore the holy city of Jerusalem back into the hands of Israel. It was during this time of intense prayer that Daniel was visited by the archangel Gabriel and was given a vision revealing the future of Israel and Jerusalem for all time. The vision was this:

> ***Daniel 9:24*** *Seventy weeks have been decreed for your people and your holy city, to finish the transgression, to make an end of sin, to make atonement for iniquity, to bring in everlasting righteousness, to seal up vision and prophecy, and to anoint the most holy [place].* ***25*** *So you are to know and discern [We see that God wanted Daniel to know and discern the timetable, the time frame, in which these future events would take place] [that] from the issuing of a decree to restore and rebuild Jerusalem until Messiah the Prince [there will be] seven weeks and sixty-two weeks; it will be built again, with plaza and moat, even in times of distress.* ***26*** *Then after the sixty-two weeks the Messiah will be cut off and have nothing, and the people of the prince who is to come will destroy the city and the sanctuary. And its end [will come] with a flood; even to the end there will be war; desolations are determined.* ***27*** *And he will make a firm covenant with the many for one week, but in the middle of the week he will put a stop to sacrifice and grain offering; and on the wing of abominations [will come] one who makes desolate [This is the 8th beast, that one-world government under the guise of the UN that will be a product of the policies, money, and directives of the United States of America, the 7th beast], even until a complete destruction, one that is decreed, is poured out on the one who makes desolate [the final beast kingdom]."* (italicized words added)

The first thing we have to understand is what is meant by seventy weeks. The term "weeks" in Scripture when used prophetically equals seven years. It is the Hebrew word *shabua* and means "a period of seven, either days or years."[13] When used prophetically throughout Scripture it usually means years, as in the book of Numbers.

> ***Numbers 14:33*** And your sons shall be shepherds for forty years in the wilderness, and they shall suffer [for] your unfaithfulness, until your corpses lie in the wilderness. ***34*** According to the number of days which you spied out the land, forty days, for every day you shall bear your guilt a year, [even] forty years, and you shall know My opposition.

When speaking of the future, God signified a day for a year, thus a "week" of days would be equal to seven years. Gabriel's message to Daniel stated "seventy weeks upon thy people and thy holy city." Seventy weeks is made up of 490 days. Thus with each day representing a year, the time period Gabriel spoke of would equal 490 years. So what is to be accomplished for Israel during these 490 years? We go back to Daniel 9:24…

> ***Daniel 9:24*** Seventy weeks have been decreed for your people and your holy city, to finish the transgression, to make an end of sin, to make atonement for iniquity, to bring in everlasting righteousness, to seal up vision and prophecy, and to anoint the most holy [place].

We need to study in detail what this Scripture means. In the phrase *"to finish the transgression,"* the word "finish" is the Hebrew word *kala* and means "to shut up, bring to an end." The word "transgression" is the word *pesha* which means "rebellion against nations, against individuals, against God." Scripture is telling us then that within 490 years, God will bring to an end Israel's rebellion against Him.

In the phrase *"to make an end of sins,"* the word "end" is the Hebrew word *taman,* and means "to finish, be at an end." "Sins" is the word *chatta'ah;* and refers to "the condition or the guilt of sin." God is telling us here that He will bring about an end of Israel's condition and guilt of sin during this same time frame.

The word "reconciliation" in *"to make reconciliation for iniquity,"* is the word *kaphar;* which means "to cover, make an atonement for," and "iniquity" is the word *avon* which means "perversity, or guilt of iniquity"[14]

God is saying in this important verse that in the time frame of 490 years, He is going to make atonement for Israel's perversity and guilt of iniquity and He will bring an end to Israel's disobedience. It is a disobedience that remains even today, in that Jews continue to reject Jesus Christ as God's only begotten Son and the Messiah. After God makes reconciliation for Israel's iniquity and when their rebellion is brought to an end, God says it will be time to *"bring in everlasting righteousness and seal up the vision and prophecy and to anoint the most Holy."* From what we have studied thus far, we can see that Daniel 9:24 says that at the end of these 490 years everlasting righteousness will be brought in by God, and it will complete the visions and prophecies of the prophets. All this will conclude with the most holy (Jesus Christ) being anointed as King of Kings and Lord of Lords. Verse 25 of Daniel 9 tells us when the last days begin.

> ***Daniel 9:25*** So you are to know and discern [that] from the issuing of a decree to restore and rebuild Jerusalem until Messiah the Prince [there will be] seven weeks and sixty-two weeks; it will be built again, with plaza and moat, even in times of distress.

This Scripture says that from a decree to restore and rebuild Jerusalem until the Messiah comes will be seven weeks and sixty-two weeks. Since a "week" is equal to seven years, seven "weeks" equals forty-nine years, and 62 "weeks" equals 434 years, making for a total of 483 years.

The decree spoken of, to restore and rebuild Jerusalem, is acknowledged by most scholars to be the 2nd decree of Artaxerxes, which was given to Nehemiah on March 14, 445 BC and is recorded in Nehemiah 2:1-8.[15] At the end of this 483 year time period, it says Messiah would come, which is exactly what happened. 483 years after the decree of Artaxerxes, which is 173,880 days using the Jewish calendar of 360 days, Jesus Christ entered into Jerusalem on a donkey and was heralded as King (John 12:13).[16]

> ***Daniel 9:26*** Then after the sixty-two weeks the Messiah will be cut off and have nothing, and the people of the prince who is to come will destroy the city and the sanctuary. And its

end *[the city and the sanctuary]* [will come] with a flood; even to the end there will be war; desolations are determined. (italicized words added)

After 483 years, the Messiah was to be cut off and have nothing. The vision Daniel received remains accurate to the minutest detail for we know from the Gospels that not many days after Jesus entered Jerusalem and was hailed as King, He was crucified and forsaken by His disciples. I would like to quote this verse from *The Amplified Bible* to further clarify this great truth.

> **Daniel 9:26(b)** And after the sixty-two weeks [of years] shall the anointed one be cut off *or* killed, and shall have nothing [and no one belonging] to [and defending] him. And the people of the *other* prince who shall come will destroy the city and the sanctuary. Its end shall come with a flood, and even to the end there shall be war, and desolations are decreed.

The "people of the other prince" is a reference to the armies of the world government that will come in the future and destroy Jerusalem during the last days. Scripture says the destruction of Jerusalem will come with a flood, which is a term used often in Scripture to depict large armies of ungodly men. The next several verses show this…

> **2 Samuel 22:5** When the waves of death compassed me, the *floods* of ungodly men made me afraid; (KJV)

> **Psalm 18:4** The sorrows of death compassed me, and the *floods* of ungodly men made me afraid. (KJV)

> **Jeremiah 46:7** Who [is] this [that] cometh up as a *flood,* whose waters are moved as the rivers?

> **Jeremiah 46:8** Egypt riseth up like *& flood,* and [his] waters are moved like the rivers; and he saith, I will go up, [and] will cover the earth; I will destroy the city and the inhabitants thereof. (KJV) (emphasis added)

These verses show how God uses the analogy of flood waters for the armies of the unrighteous. According to Scripture back in Daniel

9:26, this pillage of the holy city will continue even until the end of the last seven years, and these desolations are decreed by God to take place.

To review what has been said thus far, Daniel 9:25 and 26 told us there will be 483 years from the time of the decree to rebuild Jerusalem until Messiah comes — who at that time will be cut off, crucified, and have nothing. This portion of Scripture has already been fulfilled by Christ, so sixty-nine of the "seventy weeks" have already taken place which leaves one "week" left — which is called **the Seventieth Week of Daniel.** It is in this last seven year period that all the events of verse 26 and 27 must take place because the angel said in verse 24, **all** the events (the finishing of the transgression, the ending of sin, making atonement, and bringing in everlasting righteousness) will take place within seventy weeks or 490 years.

Why is there a gap between the sixty-ninth "week," and the yet to be fulfilled Seventieth Week? The gap is the time period of "the Church" where the world has been given the perfect opportunity to believe on the Lord Jesus Christ and be saved before the final judgments of God take place on the earth.

Let's go a step further and find out more about the event that the Word says has to take place in order for the Seventieth Week to begin.

> ***Daniel 9:27*** And he *[the beast, the other prince yet to come]* will make a firm covenant with the many for one week *[7 years],* but in the middle of the week *[which would be 3 ½ years]* he will put a stop to sacrifice and grain offering; and on the wing of abominations [will come] one who makes desolate, *[the final 8th beast, that has been brought about by the 7th]* even until a complete destruction, one that is decreed, is poured out on the one who makes desolate. (italicized words added)

Scripture says that the beast is going to make a covenant with Israel and "the many" at the beginning of the final seven year period. Three and one half years later, the beast will break this covenant and cause an abomination to be set up at the Temple Mount area that will cause not only the desolation of Jerusalem, but is going to culminate in God pouring out desolation upon this final one-world government system. What is this covenant and why does it cause such retribution not only to Israel but the whole world? The book of Genesis and the book of Isaiah give us the answer.

The Everlasting Covenant

In Genesis 12:1-3, we see God gave a promise to Abraham:

> ***Genesis 12:1*** Now the LORD said to Abraham, 'Go forth from your country, And from your relatives And from your father's house, To the land which I will show you; *2* And I will make you a great nation, And I will bless you, And make your name great; And so you shall be a blessing; *3* And I will bless those who bless you, And the one who curses you I will curse. And in you all the families of the earth shall be blessed.'

God gave Abraham a promise that would affect the entire earth, and Abraham acted on this promise from God. He left his home country and eventually settled in Canaan as recorded in Genesis 13:12, and it was in Canaan that God entered into a covenant with Abraham, promising him and his descendants the land from the River of Egypt which is on the lower west side of Israel, unto the great River Euphrates, which is on the eastern border of Iraq.

> ***Genesis 15:18*** On that day the LORD made a covenant with Abram, saying, 'To your descendants I have given this land, From the river of Egypt as far as the great river, the river Euphrates'

God also told Abraham that this covenant would be an *everlasting* covenant and that it would be established through Isaac and his descendants - *not* through the descendants of Ishmael, the son born to him by Hagar.

> ***Genesis 17:8*** 'And I will give to you and to your descendants after you, the land of your sojournings, all the land of Canaan, for an everlasting possession; and I will be their God.'

Do you see the promise? God told Abraham that the land was to be an everlasting possession.

> ***Genesis 17:19*** But God said, 'Sarah your wife shall bear you a son, and you shall call his name Isaac; and I will establish

My covenant with him for an everlasting covenant for *his descendants* after him.'

This Scripture gives the reason for the whole Middle East conflict today. God entered into an everlasting covenant with the descendants of Isaac and *they* are to inherit the land extending from the River of Egypt all the way to the Euphrates River. This covenant has not yet been realized because the descendants of Ishmael continue to live in and vie for the land that Israel presently occupies. The Bible says this whole area of land is to be owned by Isaac's descendants, Israel, and this truth was reaffirmed even to Moses in Exodus 33:1.

> ***Exodus 33:1*** Then the LORD spoke to Moses, 'Depart, go up from here, you and the people whom you have brought up from the land of Egypt, to the land of which I swore to Abraham, Isaac, and Jacob, saying, 'To your descendants I will give it.'

The land of Israel was not given to the descendants of Ishmael — those we know today as Arabs and Palestinians. Look at Joshua 1:2-4.

> ***Joshua 1:2*** Moses My servant is dead; now therefore arise, cross this Jordan, you and all this people, to the land which I am giving to them, to the sons of Israel. 3 Every place on which the sole of your foot treads, I have given it to you, just as I spoke to Moses. 4 From the wilderness and this Lebanon, even as far as the great river, the river Euphrates, all the land of the Hittites, and as far as the Great Sea toward the setting of the sun, will be your territory.

This point is worthy of emphasis because the land given in covenant by God to Israel is now being challenged and repudiated not only by the Arab world, but by Israel itself! *God promised Israel a far larger piece of land than they presently occupy today.* The land promised to Israel has since been inhabited by the descendants of Ishmael and Esau, a people who have an "everlasting enmity" towards the sons of Israel. This deep-seated hatred for God's chosen people is spoken of in Ezekiel 35:5-15.

> ***Ezekiel 35:5*** Because you have had everlasting enmity and have delivered the sons of Israel to the power of the sword at

the time of their calamity, at the time of the punishment of the end, *[the Arab world will give Israel over to the power of the sword at the time of the end]* **6** therefore, as I live, declares the Lord GOD, I will give you over to bloodshed, and bloodshed will pursue you; since you have not hated bloodshed, therefore bloodshed will pursue you. **7** And I will make Mount Seir a waste and a desolation, and I will cut off from it the one who passes through and returns.

Mount Seir, south of the Dead Sea, is representative of where the descendants of Esau lived, and these descendants of Ishmael and Esau include the Palestinians and the neighboring Arab nations. God looks upon the Arab world as enemies of His chosen people and has promised destruction and desolation to many of their cities and people in the time of the end.

What will precipitate such a crisis? Ezekiel 35:5 says the Arabs will *"deliver the sons of Israel to the power of the sword"* which will be *"at the time of the punishment of the end."* How will it happen? In Daniel 9:27 we read that the Seventieth Week of Daniel begins with Israel making a covenant with the beast (the United States) and "the many" which could represent the myriad of Arab nations around Israel. Three and a half years later, in the midst of the week, the covenant will be broken and the city of Jerusalem will be overrun by armies of ungodly men. The stage is now set for all of these events to take place for we have seen the United States relentlessly negotiate for a Palestinian state and further land concessions from Israel in order to appease and bring about peace with their Arab neighbors.

The Persian Gulf War

When Saddam Hussein began his campaign against Kuwait, the United States led the world into a worldwide mobilization of military strength via the United Nations in order to circumvent and push back (but interestingly not destroy) the threat that Saddam Hussein posed to the Middle East. President George H.W. Bush at that time said he believed the Gulf crisis to be "the crucible of the new world order." A crucible is a vessel, a cup made out of porcelain, which is used for melting, or oxidizing a substance that requires a high degree of heat. It is my firm belief that the Gulf War was the catalyst, the crucible, whereby the whole world was brought into accepting UN/US infiltration and domination into every major hot spot on the globe, and most importantly, caused Israel to fall into line with the rest of the world by accepting the means that will bring about a "new world order." By witnessing the United States' awesome military strength exerted during the Gulf crisis, Israel amazingly delegated the protection of her borders and cities over to the armies of the United States, depending on *them* to stop Iraq's missiles by way of the acclaimed Patriot missile.

As it turns out, Israel was seduced by the United States and its display of power into depending on the beast and its weaponry, rather than on God and Israel's own military might to protect their homeland. Israel forfeited her strength and belief in Jehovah's protection and instead gave it to the United States. This seduction of Israel by the United States could be seen on the White House lawn on September 13, 1993 when Israel began an initial peace plan with its sworn enemies, the Palestinians, under the assurance that the United States would be the "guarantor" of the peace process. Why was this wrong? Because Israel betrayed God by forsaking the everlasting covenant He made with Abraham and his descendants and instead, through the Oslo Peace Accord, began to formally and purposely give away land which the Palestinians have no right to own. Israel began the process of trading "land for peace" relying solely on the United States to be in President Clinton's words, the "guarantor" of its success. The promise President Clinton made to Israel was this:

> The United States is committed to ensuring that the people who are affected by this agreement will be made more secure by it, and to leading the world in marshaling the resources necessary to implement the difficult details that will make real the principles to which you commit yourselves today... Mr. Prime Minister, Mr. Chairman, this day belongs to you...Together, today, with all our hearts and all our souls, we bid them *shalom, salaam, peace.*

This initial act by Israel of forsaking the everlasting covenant and cozying up to the beast is going to have worldwide effects. Isaiah chapter 24 deals entirely with the devastation that will take place in the last days due to Israel's disobedience in this matter.

> ***Isaiah 24:1*** Behold, the LORD lays the earth waste, devastates it, distorts its surface, and scatters its inhabitants.

2 And the people will be like the priest, the servant like his master, the maid like her mistress, the buyer like the seller, the lender like the borrower, the creditor like the debtor. *3* The earth will be completely laid waste and completely despoiled, for the LORD has spoken this word. *4* The earth mourns [and] withers, the world fades [and] withers, the exalted of the people of the earth fade away. *5* The earth is also polluted by its inhabitants, for they transgressed laws, violated statutes, ***broke the everlasting covenant***. *6* Therefore, a curse devours the earth, and those who live in it are held guilty. Therefore, the inhabitants of the earth are burned, and few men are left. (emphasis added)

Israel's Covenant with Death

Leaders of Israel continue to negotiate with the Palestinians and adjacent governments about how to exchange Israeli land for the guarantee of lasting peace with their enemies who surround them. We go to Isaiah chapter 28 where it gives God's perspective of rebellious Israel in the last days when the consummate peace agreement is signed with the Arab nations:

> ***Isaiah 28:14*** Therefore, hear the word of the LORD, O scoffers, Who rule this people who are in Jerusalem, *15* Because you have said, 'We have made a covenant with death, And with Sheol we have made a pact. The overwhelming scourge will not reach us when it passes by; For we have made falsehood our refuge and we have concealed ourselves with deception.'

God calls Israel's pact with their enemies "a covenant with death." God also says that despite what Israel's leaders think, they will have in fact made falsehood their refuge and instead made a pact with the grave. The false security Israel now has by thinking the United States will protect them if attacked is going to have drastic consequences.

> ***Isaiah 28:18*** And your covenant with death shall be canceled, And your pact with Sheol shall not stand; When the overwhelming scourge passes through *[which are the attacking Arab countries]*, Then you become its trampling [place]. *19* As often as it passes through, it will seize you. For

morning after morning it will pass through, [anytime] during the day or night. And it will be sheer terror to understand what it means *[what it is saying is that Israel will then realize that they have entered into the time that is termed "Jacob's Trouble"]* **20** The bed is too short on which to stretch out, And the blanket is too small to wrap oneself in. **21** For the LORD will rise up as [at] Mount Perazim, He will be stirred up as in the valley of Gibeon; To do His task, His unusual task, And to work His work, His extraordinary work. **22** And now do not carry on as scoffers, Lest your fetters be made stronger; For I have heard from the Lord GOD of hosts, Of decisive destruction on all the earth. (italicized words added)

Because of Israel's disobedience, God will use the unbelieving nations of the world as vehicles to carry out His punishment of Israel for its rebellion, transgressions, and iniquity. This punishment that will take place during the last 3 ½ years of the Seventieth Week of Daniel is the time of *Jacob's Trouble* otherwise known as *the Great Tribulation.*

When this covenant with death is signed, the beast will break the covenant and will cause the offering of prayers and worship of the people of Israel to cease at the Temple Mount area. This event I believe will start out as a military occupation by United States led UN forces at the Temple Mount area. When the Palestinian and Syrian armies decide to move and take Jerusalem by force, the UN peace keeping force will renege on protecting Israel, just like they have done in supposedly protecting many other hot spots around the world. At that time you are going to see a flood of murder and destruction come upon the Jewish state the likes of which has never been seen before. Psalm 83 is, I believe, a prophetic utterance describing this harrowing time.

Psalm 83:1 A Song, a Psalm of Asaph. O God, do not remain quiet; Do not be silent and, O God, do not be still. *2* For, behold, Thine enemies make an uproar; And those who hate Thee have exalted themselves. *3* They make shrewd plans against Thy people, And conspire together against Thy treasured ones. *4* They have said, 'Come, and let us wipe them out as a nation, That the name of Israel be remembered no more.' *5* For they have conspired together with one mind; Against Thee do they *[the Arabs]* make a covenant: *6* The tents of Edom and the Ishmaelites; Moab, and the Hagrites; *7*

Gebal, and Ammon, and Amalek; Philistia with the inhabitants of Tyre; *8* Assyria also has joined with them; They have become a help to the children of Lot. Selah. (italicized words added)

The PLO and the Arabs have in fact conspired against Israel in order to take over that hallowed nation. It is envisioned and articulated in what is known as the "three-phase plan" adopted by the top PLO command two decades ago. In an article exposing the real motives for Yasser Arafat, the *New American* magazine described the plan:

> The first phase, from 1967 to 1974, called for shocking the world with brutal terrorist acts as a way to put the Palestinian cause before the world. Phase two, from 1974 to 1983, centered on winning political legitimacy, while continuing the "armed struggle" through separate, clandestine branches. The third phase, which we are now witnessing, is a two-part strategy for destroying Israel. The first part involves the creation of a Palestinian state (through negotiation) on territory relinquished by Israel; the second calls for using that territory to launch a final assault against the Zionist infidels.[17]

This view is substantiated by Arafat's comments in the June, 1995 issue of *Parade Magazine* when he said:

> All of us are willing to be martyrs along the way, until our flag flies over Jerusalem, the capital of Palestine. Let no one think they can scare us with weapons, for we have mightier weapons — the weapon of faith, the weapon of martyrdom, the weapon of jihad.

Also in the September, 1995 *Jerusalem Post:*

> By Allah I swear that the Palestinian people are prepared to sacrifice the last boy and the last girl so that the Palestinian flag will be flown over the walls, the churches, and the mosques of Jerusalem.

What has been the United States' role in this as the 7th beast? The United States has been deeply involved on both sides by doing the following:

#1 We give the PLO millions of dollars to build up the Gaza Strip and the West Bank and Jericho, all making Jerusalem an easier target for terrorist attacks.

#2 We offer Israel 10 billion dollars in loan guarantees as bait to keep them committed to the peace process.

#3 We send millions of dollars to a supposedly bankrupt Russia, who in turn sends weapons to Syria and Iran, both bitter enemies of Israel.

What's wrong with this picture? Nothing, if your goal as a world power is to ultimately deceive Israel and set them up for destruction. The trap is indeed being laid through an intricate web of deceit, money, and political intrigue. Israel's enemies are strengthened directly or indirectly by the United States, peace will be promised by the beast who will prove to be an unfaithful ally, and the conflagration at the holy city will begin 3 ½ years after the signing of the covenant of death, a peace treaty involving Israel and its Arab neighbors. It will be at or near this time that the famed "abomination of desolation" will take place at the Temple Mount which Jesus Christ described in Matthew 24 — the act that begins the Great Tribulation.

Betrayal and War in Jerusalem

The record in Matthew 24 begins by telling us that after Jesus left the temple with His disciples, they showed Him the buildings of the temple area. Jesus warned them not to be overly impressed with the buildings because He knew there would come a time when not one stone would be left upon another. His disciples then asked him in verse 7, *"when will this happen, and what will be the sign of your coming and the end of the age?"* Christ then proceeded to tell them the chronology of events that will take place during the last days. The first sign was a rise in the incidences of false Christ's (verse 8). Then there would be more wars and rumors of wars (verse 9), followed by a marked increase in earthquakes and famines around the world (verse 11). In verses 12-19, Christ gave His disciples added encouragement to stay faithful amidst the persecution they were going to suffer for His name. We then see what is to happen next according to the Gospel of Luke.

The Seventy Weeks of Daniel

> ***Luke 21:20*** But when you see Jerusalem surrounded by armies, then recognize that her desolation is at hand. *21* Then let those who are in Judea flee to the mountains, and let those who are in the midst of the city depart, and let not those who are in the country enter the city; *22* because these are days of vengeance, in order that all things which are written may be fulfilled.

Christ told His disciples to be aware when all these signs begin to happen — the false christs, the wars and rumors of wars, earthquakes and famines in divers places. He said when you see Jerusalem surrounded by armies — then know her desolation is at hand. This desolation is the one spoken about in Daniel 9:27 when it says in the middle of the week the beast will put a stop to sacrifice at the temple area and *"on a wing of the temple he will set up an abomination that causes desolation."* What happens next? Christ tells us in verse 23-24:

> ***Luke 21:23*** Woe to those who are with child and to those who nurse babes in those days; for there will be great distress upon the land, and wrath to this people, *24* and they will fall by the edge of the sword, and will be led captive into all the nations; and Jerusalem will be trampled underfoot by the Gentiles until the times of the Gentiles be fulfilled.

A massive slaughter will take place in Jerusalem as it is trodden down by the Gentiles (unbelieving nations) until the time of the Gentiles is fulfilled, which we will see later is speaking about the end of the Seventieth Week of Daniel. In Matthew 24, Jesus gives the same warning to flee Jerusalem that He did when He told them what to do when armies surround the city.

> ***Matthew 24:15*** Therefore when you see the abomination of desolation which was spoken of through Daniel the prophet, standing in the holy place let the reader understand, *16* then let those who are in Judea flee to the mountains; *17* let him who is on the housetop not go down to get the things out that are in his house; *18* and let him who is in the field not turn back to get his cloak. *19* But woe to those who are with child and to those who nurse babes in those days! *20* But pray that your flight may not be in the winter, or on a Sabbath; *21* for

then there will be a great tribulation, such as has not occurred since the beginning of the world until now, nor ever shall be.

These Scriptures tell us when the Great Tribulation begins. In Luke 21, Christ said when the armies surround Jerusalem, you will know the tribulation is about to begin. In Matthew 24, He says when the abomination of desolation spoken of in the book of Daniel stands in the holy place, the tribulation is about to begin. Thus, the armies surrounding Jerusalem and the abomination that makes desolate standing in the holy place are one and the same. Daniel 11:45 confirms this:

> **Daniel 11:45** And he *[the beast]* will pitch the tents of his royal pavilion between the seas and the beautiful Holy Mountain; yet he will come to his end, and no one will help him. (italicized words added)

The beast, spoken of in the last half of Daniel 11, will pitch the tents of his military forces between the seas (the Mediterranean and the Dead Sea) and the beautiful holy mountain (Jerusalem). In other words, he will station his army somewhere near or at the temple area in Jerusalem.[18] When these Gentile armies take control over the Temple Mount area, this act of arrogance and disrespect to God and the holy place will cause the beast, as God puts it, *"to come to his end and no one will help him."* It will be the beginning of the ultimate destruction of the beast through environmental and spiritual phenomena that will fully manifest itself during the final 3 ½ years of antichrist's rule.

How do we know for sure that this Gentile military presence spoken of in Daniel 11:45 is at the beginning of the Great Tribulation? We only have to read the next verse...

> **Daniel 12:1** Now at that time Michael, the great prince who stands [guard] over the sons of your people, will arise. And there will be a time of distress such as never occurred since there was a nation until that time; *[speaking about the Great Tribulation]* and at that time your people, everyone who is found written in the book, will be rescued. (italicized words added)

When this great persecution takes place, the archangel Michael will step in to help rescue the 144,000 righteous Jews and deliver them safely to Petra, situated in Edom. (Isa. 16:4; Isa. 33:15-16)

What is the Great Tribulation? **The Great Tribulation is a 3 ½ year time period of unparalleled persecution of both Jews and professing Christians.** It will begin with the abomination of desolation occurring on the Temple Mount in Jerusalem, and it will end with God's final punishment of Israel for its apostasy and rebellion toward Him. This is described in Isaiah 28:18-22:

> ***Isaiah 28:18*** And your covenant with death shall be canceled, And your pact with Sheol shall not stand; When the overwhelming scourge passes through, Then you become its trampling [place.] *19* As often as it passes through, it will seize you. For morning after morning it will pass through, [anytime] during the day or night. And it will be sheer terror to understand what it means. *20* The bed is too short on which to stretch out, And the blanket is too small to wrap oneself in. *21* For the LORD will rise up as [at] Mount Perazim, He will be stirred up as in the valley of Gibeon; To do His task, His unusual task, And to work His work, His extraordinary work *[chastising Israel through the armies of the beast]*. *22* And now do not carry on as scoffers, Lest your fetters be made stronger; For I have heard from the Lord GOD of hosts, Of decisive destruction on all the earth. (italicized words added)

How do we know this punishment will last for 3 ½ years? Look at Daniel 7:25...

> ***Daniel 7:25*** And he *[the little horn]* will speak out against the Most High and wear down the saints of the Highest One, and he will intend to make alterations in times and in law; and they will be given into his hand for a time, times, and half a time. (italicized words added)

A "time" is looked on in the Bible as a year, so this "time, times, and half a time" is the equivalent of 3 ½ years. This persecution and "wearing down of the saints" is going to take place through the changing of times and laws, thus allowing an all-out persecution to occur. This portion of Scripture I believe is being fulfilled even today with Congress and the President passing new anti-terrorism legislation in response to the terrorist attacks on our country in the past decade. Legislation in the bill from the Oklahoma City bombing provides an open door to make legal the infiltration and incarceration of those who the government decides are "questionable religious groups" or those who hold anti-big government sentiments. Citizens who are conservative, Bible-believers, or do not trust the government when it goes beyond its constitutional authority can be painted with a thick, wide brush as individuals who advocate violence and pose a threat to society. Even today, the government is leading the way with disinformation campaigns to vilify all Bible-believing Christians by connecting them with the radical fringe that espouses violence in order to "take back America." As a member of the body of Christ, you need to be clear about one thing – once we enter the Seventieth Week of Daniel there is no taking America back. America's future, and the future of the rest of the world is already written, and the future is destruction and judgment by the hand of Almighty God! Daniel 7:2 says the little horn is going to *wage war on the saints and overpower them.* Regardless of your political affiliation, the militia movement or anyone else that is what the Word of God says is going to happen and it will! What then is the proper response Christians should have toward this coming totalitarian rule? Scripture simply says,

> **Rev. 13:10** Anyone who is destined for prison will be taken to prison. Anyone destined to die by the sword will die by the sword. This means that God's holy people must endure persecution patiently and remain faithful. (NLT)

Whatever hardships await the persecuted church, it is imperative that the saints remain faithful to receive their full reward. (Rev.14:12-13)

> **Daniel 12:6** And one said to the man dressed in linen, who was above the waters of the river, 'How long [will it be] until the end of [these] wonders?' 7 And I heard the man dressed in linen, who was above the waters of the river, as he raised his right hand and his left toward heaven, and swore by Him who lives forever that it would be for a time, times, and half [a time;] and as soon as they finish shattering the power of the holy people, all these [events] will be completed.

It will take 3 ½ years for the wonders to be completed and for the beast to finish scattering the power of the holy people. We can see this also from Revelation 13:5...

> **Revelation 13:5** And there was given to him *[the beast]* a mouth speaking arrogant words and blasphemies; and authority to act for forty-two months *[3 ½ years]* was given to him. (italicized words added)

Why is it called the Great Tribulation? Because it will be the most evil and demonic time in human history. Daniel 12:1 and Matthew 24:21, Scriptures we have already read numerous times, confirm this. Why is it going to be more horrible than any other time in history? Because Satan at this time will have been thrown out of heaven permanently and he and all his evil spirits will come upon earth having great wrath. These truths are covered in Revelation 12:7-12 and Revelation 17:8.

What is the purpose of the Great Tribulation? It will serve as a punishment to unfaithful Israel and the carnal church as God uses its fire to test and refine His people.[19] Look at Jeremiah 30:11-15, speaking to Israel:

> ***Jeremiah 30:11*** 'For I am with you,' declares the LORD, 'to save you; For I will destroy completely all the nations where I have scattered you, Only I will not destroy you completely. But I will chasten you justly, And will by no means leave you unpunished.' *12* For thus says the LORD, 'Your wound is incurable, And your injury is serious. *13* There is no one to plead your cause; [No] healing for [your] sore, No recovery for you. *14* All your lovers have forgotten you, They do not seek you; For I have wounded you with the wound of an enemy, With the punishment of a cruel one, Because your iniquity is great And your sins are numerous. *15* Why do you cry out over your injury? Your pain is incurable. Because your iniquity is great And your sins are numerous, I have done these things to you.'

The Believer's Hope

What is the hope for Jews or Christians amidst this totally depressing scenario? Our hope is that we get *rescued* before the full brunt of the Great Tribulation hits. This is what God plans to do for those who are faithful to Him. Daniel 12:1 speaks of this...

> ***Daniel 12:1*** Now at that time Michael, the great prince who stands [guard] over the sons of your people, will arise. And

there will be a time of distress such as never occurred since there was a nation until that time; and at that time *[the time of the abomination of desolation of Dan. 11:45]* your people, **everyone who is found written in the book, will be rescued.** (italicized words added)

Who are these people, and what does it mean "everyone who is written in the book?" There are two groups of people that are rescued from the Great Tribulation. The first group is the 144,000 chosen Jews, made up of 12,000 from each of the twelve tribes of Israel.[20] They are rescued from the Great Tribulation and led away to safety in the wilderness. This truth is spoken of in Revelation 12:6:

> ***Revelation 12:6*** And the woman fled into the wilderness where she had a place prepared by God, so that there she might be nourished for one thousand two hundred and sixty days.

These 144,000 faithful Jews, are also known as "the woman."

> ***Revelation 12:14*** And the two wings of the great eagle were given to the woman, in order that she might fly into the wilderness to her place, where she was nourished for a time and times and half a time, *[3 ½ years, the length of the Great Tribulation]* from the presence of the serpent. (italicized words added)

Verse 15 and 16 make reference as to how Satan tries to capture this special group of Jews.

> ***Revelation 12:15*** And the serpent poured water like a river out of his mouth after the woman, so that he might cause her to be swept away with the flood.

We have already seen that armies of ungodly men were spoken of as floods. These armies will be pursuing the escaping Jews. We can read what happens to them...

> ***Revelation 12:16*** And the earth helped the woman, and the earth opened its mouth and drank up the river which the dragon poured out of his mouth.

The earth is going to open up and swallow the vast hordes of armies that will be in pursuit of God's people. I believe this event is prophetically shown in Psalm 18.

> ***Psalm 18:4*** The cords of death encompassed me, And the torrents of ungodliness terrified me. ***5*** The cords of Sheol surrounded me; The snares of death confronted me. ***6*** In my distress I called upon the LORD, And cried to my God for help; He heard my voice out of His temple, And my cry for help before Him came into His ears.

These verses tell of some of the fears the 144,000 will have as they see the armies surround their city. They cry out for help and then witness what God does to the hostile armies.

> ***Psalm 18:7*** Then the earth shook and quaked; And the foundations of the mountains were trembling And were shaken, because He was angry. ***8*** Smoke went up out of His nostrils, And fire from His mouth devoured; Coals were kindled by it. ***9*** He bowed the heavens also, and came down With thick darkness under His feet. ***10*** And He rode upon a cherub and flew; And He sped upon the wings of the wind. ***11*** He made darkness His hiding place, His canopy around Him, Darkness of waters, thick clouds of the skies. ***12*** From the brightness before Him passed His thick clouds, Hailstones and coals of fire. ***13*** The LORD also thundered in the heavens, And the Most High uttered His voice, Hailstones and coals of fire. ***14*** And He sent out His arrows, and scattered them, And lightning flashes in abundance, and routed them. ***15*** Then the channels of water appeared, And the foundations of the world were laid bare At Thy rebuke, O LORD, At the blast of the breath of Thy nostrils.

This show of power will be a spectacle beyond words as God Almighty glorifies Himself to His people.

> ***Psalm 18:16*** He sent from on high, He took me; He drew me out of many waters, ***17*** He delivered me from my strong enemy. And from those who hated me, for they were too mighty for me. ***18*** They confronted me in the day of my calamity; But the LORD was my stay. ***19*** He brought me

forth also into a broad place; He rescued me, because He delighted in me.

We see from this verse the joy the 144,000 experience after seeing God's protective power in full manifestation. The next few verses tell us *why* God saved them...

> ***Psalm 18:20*** The LORD has rewarded me according to my righteousness; According to the cleanness of my hands He has recompensed me. ***21*** For I have kept the ways of the LORD, And have not wickedly departed from my God. ***22*** For all His ordinances were before me, And I did not put away His statutes from me. ***23*** I was also blameless with Him, And I kept myself from my iniquity. ***24*** Therefore the LORD has recompensed me according to my righteousness, According to the cleanness of my hands in His eyes. ***25*** With the kind Thou dost show Thyself kind; With the blameless Thou dost show Thyself blameless; (emphasis added)

This military defeat witnessed by the world is going to cause the devil and the armies of the beast to wage war against Christians and the rest of the Jewish people with incredible vengeance.

> ***Revelation 12:17*** And the dragon was enraged with the woman, and went off to make war with the rest of her offspring, who keep the commandments of God and hold to the testimony of Jesus.

Where in the wilderness will these 144,000 Jews escape to? I believe God will cause them to flee to the ancient stone fortress of Petra, located south of the Dead Sea.[21] This can be seen from Isaiah 16...

> ***Isaiah 16:1*** Send the [tribute] lamb to the ruler of the land, From Sela, *['the rock" is Petra]* by way of the wilderness to the mountain of the daughter of Zion... ***3*** Cast your shadow like night at high noon; *[the darkness we read about in Ps. 18]* Hide the outcasts *[hide the 144,000 Jews as they flee]*, do not betray the fugitive. ***4*** Let the outcasts of Moab stay with you; Be a hiding place to them from the destroyer *[the beast]*. (italicized words added)

These "outcasts" will have a hiding place from the "destroyer," and it will be in Petra. What is so special about Petra? It is a fortress carved out of solid rock with only a narrow entrance leading into its confines — a perfect sanctuary for the 144,000 during this time of persecution.

As mentioned previously, there are two groups of people that will be rescued from the Great Tribulation. The first are the 144,000 Jews and the second group are faithful Christians, those anxiously awaiting the return of Christ. In the context of Jesus Christ speaking about the armies coming upon Jerusalem and the horrors of the tribulation period soon to come, He says in verses 34 and 35 of Luke 21...

> *Luke 21:34* Be on guard, that your hearts may not be weighted down with dissipation and drunkenness and the worries of life, and that day come on you suddenly like a trap; *35* for it will come upon all those who dwell on the face of all the earth. *36* But keep on the alert at all times, praying in order that you may have strength to **escape all these things that are about to take place, and to stand before the Son of Man.** (emphasis added)

Jesus Christ says His followers are to be alert and pray that they may be able to escape *all* these things that are about to take place and stand before the Son of man. The privilege of escaping the horrors of the Great Tribulation will come by way of "the gathering together", known also to Christians as the rapture. Jesus gave reference to this in the Gospel of Matthew.

> *Matthew 24:22*...And unless those days had been cut short *[talking about the tribulation],* no life would have been saved; but for the sake of the elect those days shall be cut short. (italicized words added)

For the sake of the elect, the days will be cut short or "amputated." Who are the elect? We already know the 144,000 are, and if we look at Luke 12:36 we can see who the elect are according to Christ.

> *Luke 12:36* And be like men who are waiting for their master when he returns from the wedding feast, so that they may immediately open [the door] to him when he comes and knocks. *[When Christ comes, these people were said to be waiting expectantly for him]* *37* Blessed are those slaves

whom the master shall find on the alert when he comes; truly I say to you, that he will gird himself [to serve] and have them recline [at the table] and will come up and wait on them. (italicized words added)

Because of a believer's anticipation and watchfulness, he will be blessed by Christ and taken care of.

Luke 12:38 Whether he comes in the second watch, or even in the third, and finds [them] so, blessed are those [slaves]. *39* And be sure of this, that if the head of the house had known at what hour the thief was coming, he would not have allowed his house to be broken into. *40* You too, be ready; for the Son of Man is coming at an hour that you do not expect *[i.e. we are to stay watchful all the time]*. *41* And Peter said, 'Lord, are You addressing this parable to us, or to everyone [else] as well?' *42* And the Lord said, 'Who then is the faithful and sensible steward, whom his master will put in charge of his servants, to give them their rations at the proper time? *[Jesus is addressing this to His disciples]* *43* Blessed is that slave whom his master finds so doing when he comes. *44* Truly I say to you, that he will put him in charge of all his possessions. *45* **But** if that slave says in his heart, 'My master will be a long time in coming,' and begins to beat the slaves, [both] men and women, and to eat and drink and get drunk; *[i.e. does not look for his master but instead gets involved in the pleasures and deceptions of the world]* *46* the master of that slave will come on a day when he does not expect [him,] and at an hour he does not know, **and will cut him in pieces, and assign him a place with the unbelievers.** (italicized words and emphasis added)

Christ's teaching is obvious. Stay oblivious to the Master and you may end up in the Great Tribulation. This Scripture also shows us that Christ cannot rapture the faithful church well into the tribulation for then it would no longer be a surprise; for even the most wayward believer will know that judgment has begun during the Great Tribulation because we are told by Christ it will be the most traumatic time in human history. It says in the above verses that the Lord's return to gather His own comes at a time when people will still be unaware, and if his servant is caught

The Seventy Weeks of Daniel

unaware and disobedient, the master will assign him a place with the unbelievers. What is that place? *It is staying on earth during the Great Tribulation.*

This amazing truth is laid out by Jesus Christ Himself as He addresses the seven churches in the first three chapters of the book of Revelation. Of all the churches addressed and chastised by the Lord for various levels of unbelief and unfaithfulness, Jesus Christ stops and gives only the church of Philadelphia this most wonderful and amazing promise:

> ***Revelation 3:7*** And to the angel of the church in Philadelphia write: He who is holy, who is true, who has the key of David, who opens and no one will shut, and who shuts and no one opens, says this: *8* I know your deeds. Behold, I have put before you an open door which no one can shut, because you have a little power, and have kept My word, and have not denied My name. *9* Behold, I will cause [those] of the synagogue of Satan, who say that they are Jews, and are not, but do lie; behold, I will make them to come and bow down at your feet, and to know that I have loved you. *10* **Because you have kept the word of My perseverance, I also will keep you from the hour of testing, that [hour] which is about to come upon the whole world, to test those who dwell upon the earth.**

Jesus Christ says in verse 10, because these faithful believers have kept His word, He also will keep them from the hour of testing, that hour of testing which is about to come upon the whole world. What is the hour of testing? The Great Tribulation. Before we go any further, let's make sure we understand the meaning of these words.

Protected by God

The word "kept" is the word *tereo,* which means "attend to carefully, to guard, to watch over." Because those in the church of Philadelphia had kept, guarded and held fast to Christ's words, He says, "I also will keep you *[tereo]* from *[ek]* the hour of testing." This word *ek* is explained in *The Companion Bible* by E.W. Bullinger.

> *Ek* governs only one case (the Genitive) and it denotes motion from the interior. It is used of time, place, and origin.

It means "out from", as distinguished from *apo* which means "off," or "away from"...[22]

Jesus Christ told the church of Philadelphia that because of their perseverance, He will keep and protect them from the interior of the Great Tribulation.

The word "testing" is the word *peirasmos* which means "temptation or putting to the proof." The Great Tribulation will be the "mother of all testing grounds," not only in terms of persecution for those who want to believe the Bible, but from temptations so strong and so beguiling that if possible they will deceive even the very elect. Those who are spared that testing are those who have already shown themselves to be faithful to Christ and His Word.

How will the faithful be raptured? By surprise, and before the full fury of the Great Tribulation begins.

> ***Matthew 24:36*** But of that day and hour no one knows, not even the angels of heaven, nor the Son, but the Father alone. ***37*** For the coming of the Son of Man will be just like the days of Noah. ***38*** For as in those days which were before the flood they were eating and drinking, they were marrying and giving in marriage, until the day that Noah entered the ark, ***39*** and *they did not understand until the flood came and took them all away*; so shall the coming of the Son of Man be. ***40*** Then there shall be two men in the field; one will be taken, and one will be left. ***41*** Two women [will be] grinding at the mill; one will be taken, and one will be left. ***42*** Therefore be on the alert, for you do not know which day your Lord is coming. ***43*** But be sure of this, that if the head of the house had known at what time of the night the thief was coming, he would have been on the alert and would not have allowed his house to be broken into. ***44*** For this reason you be ready too; for the Son of Man is coming at an hour when you do not think [He will.] (emphasis added)

Christ made His coming analogous to a thief in the night. A thief comes in unawares, *takes what is valuable,* and then leaves. That is what Christ will do in the rapture. He will come by stealth, grab His faithful church, and leave the carnal, unfaithful church to be tested *[peraismos]* by way of the Great Tribulation.

This record of "one will be taken the other left" coincides perfectly with the suddenness of the rapture as stated in 1 Thessalonians 4:16-17 and 1 Corinthians 15:51-52.

1 Thessalonians 4:16 For the Lord Himself will descend from heaven with a shout, with the voice of [the] archangel, and with the trumpet of God; and the dead in Christ shall rise first. *17* Then we who are alive and remain shall be caught up together with them in the clouds to meet the Lord in the air, and thus we shall always be with the Lord.

1 Corinthians 15:51 Behold, I tell you a mystery; we shall not all sleep, but we shall all be changed, *52* in a moment, in the twinkling of an eye, at the last trumpet; for the trumpet will sound, and the dead will be raised imperishable, and we shall be changed.

But how do we *really know* we will be taken out before all hell breaks loose? Look at Luke 17:26-37.

Luke 17:26 And just as it happened in the days of Noah, so it shall be also in the days of the Son of Man: *27* they were eating, they were drinking, they were marrying, they were being given in marriage, until the day that Noah entered the ark, and the flood came and destroyed them all. *[Noah and his family were safe first, then the wrath came]* *28* It was the same as happened in the days of Lot: they were eating, they were drinking, they were buying, they were selling, they were planting, they were building; *[life was still relatively normal on earth at this time]* *29* but on the day that Lot went out from Sodom it rained fire and brimstone from heaven and destroyed them all. *[God escorted Lot to safety before He rained down judgment]* *30* It will be just the same on the day that the Son of Man is revealed. *31* On that day, let not the one who is on the housetop and whose goods are in the house go down to take them away; and likewise let not the one who is in the field turn back. *[This is the same admonition that Christ gave when he spoke of the armies surrounding Jerusalem at the time of the abomination of desolation]* *32* Remember Lot's wife. *33* Whoever seeks to keep his life shall lose it, and whoever loses [his life] shall preserve it. *34*

> I tell you, on that night there will be two men in one bed; one will be taken, and the other will be left, *[the gathering together of the faithful church]* **35** There will be two women grinding at the same place; one will be taken, and the other will be left. **36** Two men will be in the field; one will be taken and the other will be left. **37** And answering they said to Him, 'Where, Lord?' And He said to them, 'Where the body [is], there also will the vultures be gathered.' (italicized words added)

These are comforting verses for the born-again believer who is faithfully standing and waiting for the Lord's return. There is a sad side to Christ's return though, and it is addressed many times by Jesus Christ through the use of parables — stories that illustrate profound truth. We see such an instance in Luke 12:35.

> ***Luke 12:35*** Be dressed in readiness, and [keep] your lamps alight... *[Christ goes on to speak about the faithful slave who was alert and waiting for his master]* **45** But if that slave says in his heart, 'My master will be a long time in coming,' *[remember this is referring not to an unbeliever, but one who was serving his Master]* and begins to beat the slaves, [both] men and women, and to eat and drink and get drunk; **46** the master of that slave will come on a day when he does not expect [him,] and at an hour he does not know, and will cut him in pieces, and assign him a place with the unbelievers. **47** And that slave who knew his master's will and did not get ready or act in accord with his will, shall receive many lashes... (italicized words added)

The slave, or in this case, the believer in Christ, who neither expects nor desires his Master's return and continues in flagrant disobedience will find that his portion is with the unbelievers during the tribulation period. In Matthew 24, Christ speaks solely about the end of the age and at the end of the chapter He urges His disciples to be ready and alert for His return. He then continues to teach on the same theme throughout Matthew 25 with more parables.[23] For instance, the parable of the ten virgins...

> ***Matthew 25:1*** Then the kingdom of heaven will be comparable to ten virgins, who took their lamps, and went

out to meet the bridegroom. *2* And five of them were foolish, and five were prudent. *3* For when the foolish took their lamps, they took no oil with them, *4* but the prudent took oil in flasks along with their lamps *[they were ready and prepared]*. *5* Now while the bridegroom was delaying, they all got drowsy and [began] to sleep. *6* But at midnight there was a shout, 'Behold, the bridegroom! Come out to meet [him.'] *7* Then all those virgins rose, and trimmed their lamps. *8* And the foolish said to the prudent, 'Give us some of your oil, for our lamps are going out.' *9* But the prudent answered, saying, 'No, there will not be enough for us and you [too;] go instead to the dealers and buy [some] for yourselves.' *10* And while they were going away to make the purchase, the bridegroom came, and those who were ready went in with him to the wedding feast; and the door was shut *[the rapture]*. *11* And later the other virgins also came, saying, 'Lord, lord, open up for us.' *12* But he answered and said, 'Truly I say to you, I do not know you.'

In the eyes of Christ, "getting it together" spiritually at the last minute after you have been sleeping around with the rest of the world is not going to work. He says this in Matthew 7:21-27...

Matthew 7:21 Not everyone who says to Me, 'Lord, Lord,' will enter the kingdom of heaven; but he who does the will of My Father who is in heaven. *22* Many will say to Me on that day, 'Lord, Lord, did we not prophesy in Your name, and in Your name cast out demons, and in Your name perform many miracles?' *23* And then I will declare to them, 'I never knew you; depart from Me, you who practice lawlessness. *24* Therefore everyone who hears these words of Mine, and acts upon them, may be compared to a wise man, who built his house upon the rock. *25* And the rain descended, and the floods came, and the winds blew, and burst against that house; and [yet] it did not fall, for it had been founded upon the rock. *26* And everyone who hears these words of Mine, and does not act upon them, will be like a foolish man, who built his house upon the sand. *27* And the rain descended, and the floods came, and the winds blew, and burst against that house; and it fell, and great was its fall.

From the words uttered by the Lord Himself, every Christian should look within their heart and ask themselves the questions — "Am I part of the church of Philadelphia?" "Have I kept, guarded, and held fast to Christ's words in my life?" "Am I looking for and anxiously awaiting His return, or am I tied to and in love with this world?" If you are a Christian and have taken the sacrifice of Christ lightly by relegating your life to one of silence and indifference to the things of God, I urge you, as a brother in Christ, to seriously ponder this message. Jesus Christ our Master is coming soon. Are you ready and watching? If not, prepare now so you will not have to face *"that hour which is about to come upon the whole world, to test those who dwell upon the earth."* (Rev. 3:10)

Chapter 4

The Man of Sin Revealed

The book of 2 Thessalonians provides important insight from the church epistles as to when and how the rapture of the faithful church takes place.

> *2 Thessalonians 2:1* Now we beseech you, brethren, by the coming of our Lord Jesus Christ, and [by] our gathering together unto him, *2* That ye be not soon shaken in mind, or be troubled, neither by spirit, nor by word, nor by letter as from us, as that the day of Christ is at hand. (KJV)

Paul is imploring these faithful believers that they need **not** be shaken or fearful concerning the wrath of God because key factors concerning the return of Christ had yet to occur. Why is this consoling? Because it says the timing of the rapture will rescue the true believer from the evil days of the Great Tribulation and the vengeful reign of the final eighth beast empire. This we will see as we go through the powerful chapter verse by verse.

The word "coming" in verse one is the Greek word *parousia,* which means "a being along side of, a presence." The word "gathering together" is the word *epinouge* and refers to "a gathering together in one place." This being alongside and being in the presence of the Lord Jesus Christ is the hope that Paul wanted the saints in Thessalonica to steel their minds on, for it is this hope, of being gathered together with Christ, that remains the foundation stone to keep believers free from fear as the days grow darker ahead. The New International Version reads *"...not to become easily unsettled or alarmed by some prophecy, report or letter supposed to have come from us, saying that the day of the Lord has already come."* This verse can be perceived and interpreted in a number of ways. The Stephens Greek text from which the King James Version is translated has "that the day of Christ *[christos]* is at hand." Other translations render the passage as saying that the day of the Lord is at hand, or has already come.

A key point to understand is that "the day of Christ" is spoken of as a time of joy and exaltation in the epistles (1 Cor. 1:7, 8; Phil. 1:6; Phil 2:16), for we will be safe and at home with the Lord. The words, "Day of the Lord" however bear a totally different connotation, one of fearful wrath and judgment being poured out not only on unbelievers, but on Israel as well. This will be the time the trumpet judgments begin, just after the manifestation of the sixth seal. Through this one manifestation, that of the sun turning black and the moon turning red like blood, those who remain on earth will know that the Day of the Lord has begun (Rev. 6:12-17).

It seems what was happening to the church in Thessalonica was that they were being told by false or deceived brethren that the Day of Christ (the rapture) had already come, and thus they assumed they were left on earth to suffer through what they knew to be the horrible Day of the Lord judgments. Paul encouraged them not to be deceived by such lies from him or anyone else, and he informed them that the Day of Christ, the day that pertains to their gathering unto Him, would *not* come until the apostasy comes first, and the man of sin who is the son of destruction is revealed. Paul reminds them that the "man of lawlessness" will have to reveal himself first and proclaim himself as God. This truth was exactly what Paul was alluding to when he said, "when I was with you, did I not tell you these things?" He spoke these same truths in his first letter to the Thessalonians. In 1 Thessalonians, chapter 4, Paul lays out the hope of how Christ will return.

> ***I Thessalonians 4:16*** For the Lord himself shall descend from heaven with a shout, with the voice of the archangel, and with the trump of God: and the dead in Christ shall rise first: ***17*** Then we which are alive [and] remain shall be caught up together with them in the clouds, to meet the Lord in the air: and so shall we ever be with the Lord. ***18*** Wherefore comfort one another with these words. (KJV)

Paul goes on in 1 Thessalonians chapter 5 about a time when the unbelieving world will be saying "peace and safety," a time most likely near the abomination of desolation when *man* proclaims his sovereignty over Jerusalem as the false messiah of peace. When that occurs and the surrounding Arab nations attack Jerusalem, destruction will fall swiftly and by God's intervening hand He will destroy a portion of the Arab armies. At this point God will also miraculously deliver the 144,000 Jews to safety in Edom and the severity of the Great Tribulation will begin to be unleashed on the earth forcing the rest of Israel and all those of the unfaithful church, to make the choice whether or not they will "hold to the testimony of Jesus." Paul encourages the faithful brethren in Thessalonica, as well as every other faithful believer, to not fear that day, for God has not destined them to wrath but for the obtaining of salvation by our Lord and Savior Jesus Christ at the rapture.

Think through these events from what we already know from Scripture. Persecution will begin to escalate against the faithful church and Israel during the first 3 ½ years of the Seventieth Week of Daniel. We are beginning to see glimpses of that take place today. 2 Timothy 3:1-5 also speaks of the atmosphere that will prevail in society and among the church as we continue to move into "the last days."

> *2 Timothy 3:1* This know also, that in the last days perilous times shall come. *2* For men shall be lovers of their own selves, covetous, boasters, proud, blasphemers, disobedient to parents, unthankful, unholy, *3* Without natural affection, trucebreakers, false accusers, incontinent, fierce, despisers of those that are good, *4* Traitors, heady, high-minded, lovers of pleasures more than lovers of God; *5* Having a form of godliness, but denying the power thereof: from such turn away. (KJV)

The case could be made that this verse is rapidly coming to pass if not already here. Also look what will be happening in these times...

> *2 Timothy 4:3* For the time will come when they will not endure sound doctrine; but after their own lusts shall they heap to themselves teachers, having itching ears; *4* And they shall turn away [their] ears from the truth, and shall be turned unto fables. (KJV)

Today, teachers and ministers have gotten further and further away from the gospel of Jesus Christ and as a result many churches are falling into apostasy and rejection of the truth. This apostasy, the ripening of people's minds for the acceptance of antichrist, will continue unabated as we draw near to the Great Tribulation so the persecution of people who "hold to the testimony of Jesus" can successfully be carried out. First Thessalonians, chapter 5 shows us being delivered from the darkness and wrath that will descend on earth because we will be rescued — raptured away by the return of Christ. With this backdrop in mind, let us continue to read in 2 Thessalonians 2:3-4.

> *2 Thessalonians 2:3* Let no man deceive you by any means: for [that day shall not come], except there come a falling away first, and that man of sin be revealed, the son of perdition; *4* Who opposeth and exalteth himself above all that is called God, or that is worshipped; so that he as God sitteth in the temple of God, shewing himself that he is God. (KJV)

The word "man" in "man of sin" is the word *anthropos,* which means "men of the human race, a generic term speaking of mankind in general."[24] The word "sin" is the noun form of the word *hamartia,* and means "the complex of sins committed by either a single person or by many, i.e. lawlessness."[25]

We know that given what 2 Timothy 3:1-7 says about the hearts of men on earth at this time, this "man of sin" is not just speaking about one man who is lawless, but could include society in general which will have continued to move towards ever greater depravity and rebelliousness towards God. People who have stood for the gospel in the past will become disillusioned and depart from the faith. Great evil will begin to prevail throughout the world as people succumb to the evil one and reject the light of God's Word. This surge of apostasy will be epitomized when the leader of the beast (a.k.a. antichrist) along with the armies behind him, claim jurisdiction and authority over Jerusalem in the name of peace. This attitude of total defiance and blasphemy against God will be revealed as the beast stands in utter defiance to the everlasting covenant that God set up with the descendants of Israel. For this travesty and abominable sin, God calls him the "son of perdition," the word "son" being the word *huios* which deals specifically regarding origin and nature. The "son of perdition," due to his disobedience and hate for the truth is doomed to destruction, which is exactly what perdition means. It is the word *apoleia,* and means "an utter and final ruin which cannot be reversed upon all those who do not believe the truth." (Rev. 17:8,11; 2 Pet. 3:7; 2 Thess. 2:10-12; 2 Thess. 1:7-9.)

How will this happen? It will happen when the leader of the beast, and all the people who are falling into lockstep to the beast's agenda, exalt themselves by opposing God's specific will in the Middle East which is for Israel to not give away any of their land to the Palestinian or Arab world.

2 Thessalonians 2:3 Let no man deceive you by any means: for [that day shall not come], except there come a falling away first, and that man of sin be revealed, the son of perdition; ***4*** Who opposeth and exalteth himself above all that is called God, or that is worshipped; so that he as God sitteth in the temple of God, shewing himself that he is God.

In verse four it says that the man of sin takes his seat in the temple of God, showing himself that he is God. It is important to note here that the word used for temple in this verse is the Greek word *naos,* which can refer to a person's body and heart (Jn. 2:19). It is not the word *herion,* which is used to describe the physical temple in Jerusalem. The all-important truth to realize in verse four is that the man of sin reaches such a humanistic and self-absorbed state of mind in his "temple" that he blatantly and brazenly defies the sovereign will of God. This awesome and blasphemous act will take place at the Temple Mount area in Jerusalem as representatives of mankind choose to regard themselves as God in solving the crisis about Israel's future.

The "abomination of desolation," or termed another way, the abomination that makes desolate, will serve as the ignition point for Satan to have his way against wayward Israel and reprobate Christians for it will be at this time that the purging and punishment of mankind will take place throughout the world.

Man elevating himself to this level of prominence in his own mind can be perfectly seen in Ezekiel 28:2-9 where the prince of Tyre, a character unknown to Bible historians, takes on all the unsavory characteristics that Lucifer himself did when he became lifted up with pride due to his beauty and magnificence. This usurpation of pride and arrogance is why the Lord will punish the beast with utter destruction for he will be attempting to subvert the worship of Almighty God. Second Thessalonians 2:6 begins to take us into truths the church vitally needs to know.

2 Thessalonians 2:6 And now ye know what withholdeth that he might be revealed in his time. (KJV)

Paul was reminding the Thessalonians of a truth he had told them before as evidenced by his statement, *"And ye know what witholdeth that he might be revealed."* We were not privy to the special times of fellowship in which Paul must have shared these valuable truths, so we are left in a quandary as to just who this "he that witholdeth" is. There are many views and theories about who the "he" is referring to, whether it is Satan up in heaven before he gets expelled at the beginning of the tribulation, or whether it is speaking of the church, the Body of Christ in that they spiritually "keep" the earth from putrefying through the preserving effect they have on the world as the "salt of the earth." I prefer to go with the latter view for 3 simple reasons.

1. The context of the verses around it.
2. The context of the chapter as a whole, being one of hope.
3. The context of what truth Paul had mentioned to them previously in 1 Thessalonians.

Paul was inspired by God to teach the Thessalonians about the hope of being raptured and then to explain the judgment that will fall on unbelieving mankind. He did this because the Thessalonians were the faithful church, the only church whose epistle has no reproof — a point reminiscent of the those in the church of Philadelphia in Revelation 3:10 who though little in strength, were faithful to Christ's words and were told they would be spared the hour of testing, "that hour that shall come upon the face of the earth."

The word "witholdeth" in verse six means "to hold down or restrain." Paul taught the brethren that they served as a restrainer on the forces of evil and as they stayed faithful, they were keeping the forces of darkness at bay until man reaches such a state of lawlessness and apostasy towards God that they would accept the apex of evil — the dominance of the final beast empire. The situation is similar to the times of Noah and the times of Lot. They endured living amongst tremendous evil until it got so bad that God pulled them out of harm's way before He destroyed the wicked.

The "man of sin" will be revealed in his fullness when the abomination of desolation takes place in Jerusalem, when the armies of the nations under the leadership and guise of the beast, will seek to establish and declare rule over Jerusalem and the sacred temple area.

> *2 Thessalonians 2:7* For the mystery of iniquity doth already work: only he who now letteth [will let], until he be taken out of the way. (KJV)

The Man of Sin Revealed

This mystery of iniquity that was already at work in Paul's time is referring to the pathways whereby Satan guides men to rebel against God and against His Christ.

Psalm 2:1 *Why do the heathen rage, and the people imagine a vain thing?* ***2*** *The kings of the earth set themselves, and the rulers take counsel together, against the LORD, and against his anointed, [saying],* ***3*** *Let us break their bands asunder, and cast away their cords from us.* ***4*** *He that sitteth in the heavens shall laugh: the Lord shall have them in derision.* ***5*** *Then shall he speak unto them in his wrath, and vex them in his sore displeasure.* (KJV)

Ever since Adam and Eve, Satan has been intricately involved in deceiving and manipulating men into carrying out his pernicious ways against all those who oppose him. King Herod was a prime example of this manipulation in that he was used as a tool by Satan to attempt to destroy the Christ child and subvert the counsel of God. Government leaders continue to be used by the devil to persecute, obfuscate, and ultimately crush God's message of hope and salvation that comes through the preaching of the gospel of Christ.

How all this is accomplished is where a fascinating and winding trail begins. Bookshelves today are full of well documented histories about how secret societies and theosophical think-tanks have over the ages sought to bring the peoples of the world under their autocratic and humanistic control. Domination over the theology and methodology by which the world runs is their ultimate and final goal. Though many of these conspirators may believe they are carrying out their *own* goals of self-aggrandizement, they are merely pawns, stooges, for the ruthless and merciless aims of Satan whose goal is to annihilate all remnants of the seed of Abraham and those who hold to the testimony of Jesus. Satan, knowing that his days are numbered before receiving the final crushing blow of defeat by the hand of God, is purposely working through men of power to subject the world to an authoritarian nightmare — a time of antichrist — when Christianity and belief in the one true God will mean certain and brutal death. The past flames of persecution as carried out by deceived religious leaders through the Inquisition all the way to this century's slaughter of millions through the iron hand of Communism, all serve as mere forerunners to what Satan has in store in what Christ referred to as *"that day in which there hasn't been nor ever shall be."* (Matt. 24:21)

But why the sense of urgency now? Why do biblical Christians sense that time is running out and the time of God's judgment is at hand? It is because despite the marvels of modern technology and its ability to spread the gospel like never before, the darkness that prevails over men's minds is beginning to close in and suffocate any real repentance in men's and women's hearts. The affluent, developed countries of this world are becoming more immersed in materialism and sensuality and with that comes an ever growing indifference to the true gospel of peace encapsulated by repentance and salvation through Jesus Christ and His atoning blood. The lies have been laid. The death producing philosophy of the adversary has been successfully sold. **Man** controls his own destiny. **Man** is the one to bring about peace, and *he* is the sole arbitrator over the affairs of men. This lie from hell has been swallowed and promulgated by virtually every politician in that they see man as capable of solving his own problems instead of repenting of his own ways and seeking the ways of the Lord as found in Scripture. Even a moralistic coalition of legislators who refuse to speak out in public about the relevance and dire need for people to come back to the Scriptures remain part of the problem instead of the solution. God, and our total dependence on Him, needs to be addressed and recognized by everyone if our governments are to survive. There is no doubt in my mind that if Jesus Christ Himself were to walk the streets of the United States today, He would be lampooned and ridiculed by the mainstream press and prominent politicians alike as a right-wing, extremist kook — a radical ideologue whose voice needed to be squelched.

This ever emerging apostasy of the things of God by many of our leaders is what 2 Thessalonians 2:7 is talking about.

> ***2 Thessalonians 2:7*** For the mystery of iniquity doth already work...

The "mystery of iniquity," this deliberate and calculated subversion of all the truths contained in the Bible, was at work back in Paul's day and is at work today.

> ... only he who now letteth [will let], until he be taken out of the way. (KJV)

Who is the "he" referring to? The word "letteth" is the Greek word *katecho* and means "to restrain, to hinder the course or progress of." It is my belief that "he" is the restraining power of the believing church, those who are God's children under the power of the Holy Spirit who continue to make a point of standing and speaking the unadulterated Word of God. It says these believers are restraining, or hindering the devil from being fully manifest, until the final eighth beast becomes manifest. When does this "mystery of iniquity" become fully known? *"Only he who now letteth [will let], until he be taken out of the way."*

Satan's full, diabolical self will become known when the believers of the faithful church are "taken out of the way." The word "out of" is the Greek word *ek* which means "out of, away from," and the word "way" is the Greek word *mesos* which means "in the middle, in the midst of." This powerful Scripture is actually a description of the rapture itself!

> **2 Thessalonians 2:7** The mystery of iniquity doth already work, only he *[the faithful believer]* who now letteth *[restrains the mystery of iniquity]* will let *[restrain]* until he *[the faithful believer]* be taken out of the way *[by way of the rapture]*. (KJV) (italicized words added)

Here we see God's grace. The faithful church on earth is restraining, holding down the forces of evil as Satan and his manipulative army begins to gain speed in their seduction of men. At the specific time God sees man no longer wants to receive the message of the gospel, He will gather the faithful church "out of the midst" of the world to forever be joined with Him, "kept" by His power and love from the hour of testing that will then descend upon the earth.

This testing will come by Satan being cast down permanently from heaven (Rev. 12:7-12), resulting in his anger and attacks being directed at Jews and those carnal and unrepentant Christians who refused to listen to Christ's admonitions about how to prepare oneself for His coming as described in the first three chapters of Revelation. This time of testing, the *periasmos,* will be a test to purge and refine those believers who merely gave lip service to the King of Kings and Lord of Lords. Their ultimate fate rests in *their* hands as to whether or not they will succumb to the dire temptations and ploys that will be rampant at the time of the Great Tribulation.

This rescue of the faithful church from the imploding havoc due to descend upon earth is likened by Jesus to when God rescued Lot from

Sodom and Gomorrah before His angels carried out their destructive mission. God will do the same for all those who seek to love and serve Him and choose not to be allured by the lusts and pleasures of this world.

It is after this divine rescue of both the faithful church and the 144,000 elect, that God will allow Satan to successfully and mercilessly torture the rest of the idolatrous church so that they repent. Through such chastisement, God will show that He is both a jealous God and a righteous Judge; a God who demands obedience and sovereignty over every person's life.

This profound, yet accurate truth can be seen in the way the Pharisees, so sanctimonious and satanically driven (Jn. 8:43-44), were actually used by God to bring about God's ultimate will for mankind; the crucifixion and death of our Lord and Savior Jesus Christ (Matt. 26:39). God will again use, in His own omnipotent way, the persecution performed by Satan and his minions to unwittingly purge and refine His wayward church into recognizing the Lordship and authority of His Son, Jesus Christ. The purging of 3 ½ years during the Great Tribulation will force both Jews and Christians to reevaluate their lives and their allegiance to God to the point that they will decide whether they want to serve the Savior, the Lord Jesus Christ, or the god of this fallen world, Satan. Verse eight goes on to describe what will take place during this time.

> ***2 Thessalonians 2:8*** And then shall that Wicked be revealed, whom the Lord shall consume with the spirit of his mouth, and shall destroy with the brightness of his coming: (KJV)

Who is this that the Lord shall consume with the spirit of His mouth? It is the eighth beast — a world government that will be led ultimately by a person who will personify and be completely indwelt by Satan. This terrifying event will occur sometime at, or near the time of the rapture when Satan is cast down permanently from heaven and is no longer able to accuse the brethren before the Lord. Upon his expulsion, Satan will channel his full energy and power within "the Wicked one" (*ananomos;* lawless one, transgressor) and it will become evident to all on the earth that the power driving this new world government is in fact hurtling mankind into an abyss of confusion, darkness and despair. Second Thessalonians describes the Wicked One.

2 Thessalonians 2:9 [Even him], whose coming is after the working of Satan with all power and signs and lying wonders, (KJV)

He will be the culmination of Satan's ideology, a promoter of fear, hate, and rejection of God's commands in trade for worship of self. This coming world government, due to the working of Satan, will be fueled by what the Apostle Paul saw as power, signs and lying wonders — many of the same "miracles" that the Apostle John saw in Revelation 13 that caused people to worship the beast. These "miracles" include all the technological wonders that have propelled our nation into becoming the superpower and economic giant of the world today, but there will likely be more. Along with these "wonders," the further seduction of people around the world will continue as Satan moves among the disciples of New Age mysticism to begin to look for and expect environmental and extraterrestrial phenomena to take place soon. The expectation by present New Agers of looming climactic changes has been woven into a masterful disinformation campaign that predicts environmental holocaust due to man's pillage of "Mother Earth's" resources and global warming. The fear of all "enlightened" New Agers is now environmental and global suicide due in their minds *not* to God's impending judgment, but because of the supposed disastrous effects civilization has had on its "fellow animals."

These predictions all accurately represent what the Bible says lie ahead when the birth pangs of God's judgment become manifest when the third and fourth seals of Revelation are opened. The lying signs and wonders that will take place according to 2 Thessalonians 2:9 will be used to deceive those seeking answers why thousands of Christians have vanished via the rapture and why cataclysmic things are happening on earth. Satan will say through his deceivers that such phenomena means man is at the threshold of reaching his ultimate fulfillment as an all-powerful entity, when in reality the cosmic and environmental signs will be heralding that certain doom awaits mankind in the not too distant future.

What is our hope? God through His infinite love and grace spells out to the faithful church in Thessalonica the hope that every true born-again believer should look for. We can expect to see a falling away of the church, military occupation by US/UN coalition forces in the temple area of Jerusalem, and a pronouncement by the beast's forces that they will rule and protect Jerusalem's divine interests. When this blatant

REVELATION UNRAVELED

pronouncement takes place, faithful believers will find themselves catapulted into glory by the rapture as unbelieving mankind is left to suffer under the hands of antichrist. Where will you choose to be?

Chapter 5

A Comparison of the Words of Christ

Jesus Christ is King of kings and Lord of lords. He is the image of the invisible God, the first born of all creation (Col. 1:15). He is also the head of the church (Col. 1:18), the resurrection and the life in that whosoever believeth in Him shall never die. If that is what the Bible says, then why do we not hear what He says? That is my concern for all those who get carried away into the deceptive theology of hyper-dispensationalism[26] and set aside parts of the four Gospels and the book of Revelation as inconsequential to the church because they are supposedly addressed only to Israel. This dangerous attitude subtly relegates Jesus Christ to the position of a mere prophet instead of being the living, incarnate Word of God. I believe strict dispensationalists commit a catastrophic error when they sit in judgment over which of Jesus' words to apply to themselves for they forget it will be the Lord Jesus Himself who will judge them for every idle word they speak.[27]

Where, after all, does one learn initially about Jesus Christ? Does the unbeliever turn to the church epistles? No, he turns to the Gospels to learn more about the Savior who lived and died for our sins and who promised He would return again. Jesus said *"the words that I speak unto you are spirit and they are life."* That means ALL OF THEM. How could His words be addressed only to Israel seeing He spoke truths regarding all eternity and commanded His disciples to go and teach everyone throughout the world all the things He had taught them? When Christ gave the Great Commission He had to be referring to the principles and truths taught in the Gospels for the revelation contained in the church epistles did not even start to be revealed until some twenty years after Christ's resurrection. It was also during the teaching of the early church that the Lord abundantly confirmed the Word of the apostles with signs, miracles and wonders.[28]

Why does this theological twisting even come about? Because seminaries and intellectuals have a profound knack for taking something very simple and making it extremely complex. They have a habit of putting layer upon layer of theological juxtapositions on the parables and the truths that Christ spoke but every supposition they add only amounts to foolishness as men try to improve on an already perfect Word. We need to just believe what Christ said. After all, who are we to change or challenge His words? He always spoke and did the will of the Father.[29]

While on earth, Jesus did not seek out the company of the pious and scholarly Pharisees, but instead chose to give His message straight and true - in ways common people could understand. It was this ability to distill eternal truths into simple stories and analogies that angered the top religious leaders against the Lord because they saw their own renown as "spiritual heavies" evaporate, a situation no intellectual can bear.

The truth is that Jesus Christ spoke forth what signs would precede His second coming to His disciples and He reiterated these truths in detailed fashion as He spoke to the seven churches in the book of Revelation.

Chapter 24 of the Gospel of Matthew stands as a bulwark of prophetic truth, and it is in this chapter that Christ sets forth the litany of events that will take place preceding His glorious return. Later in the record, He goes on to further document and illustrate how these events will take place by using parables, thus making sure that no mistakes are made how these magnificent truths are to be understood. We begin the record…

> ***Matthew 24:1*** And Jesus came out from the temple and was going away when His disciples came up to point out the temple buildings to Him.

A few days before being delivered by the Jews to be slain by Roman hands, Jesus came out of the temple area and was asked to glory along with His disciples at the magnificence of the buildings that made up the Temple Mount area. What was Jesus' response?

> ***Matthew 24:2*** And He answered and said to them, 'Do you not see all these things? Truly I say to you, not one stone here shall be left upon another, which will not be torn down.'

Jesus obviously knew something the disciples didn't. He knew all these buildings would be torn down and become rubble, but it was not because He had an inside tip on the Romans destroying it in 70 AD. He knew that something bigger would occur and the time frame is defined by

A Comparison of the Words of Christ

the disciple's question: *"When shall these things* [the destruction of the temple] *be, and what will be the sign of your coming and the end of the age?"* Jesus answers their question in Luke, chapter 21:

> ***Luke 21:6*** [As for] these things which you are looking at, the days will come in which there will not be left one stone upon another which will not be torn down.

Was Jesus referring to when the Romans would come level it? No, for we see in the next three verses that the context has it leading up to the end times.

> ***Luke 21:7*** And they questioned Him, saying, 'Teacher, when therefore will these things be? And what [will be] the sign when these things are about to take place?' *8* And He said, 'See to it that you be not misled; for many will come in My name, saying, 'I am [He,'] and, 'The time is at hand'; do not go after them. *9* And when you hear of wars and disturbances, do not be terrified; for these things must take place first, but the end [does] not [follow] immediately.' (emphasis added)

If you read the rest of the chapter, you will see that Jesus set the destruction to be sometime during the Great Tribulation. I believe that Jesus knew from the book of Ezekiel that in the times of the end every wall, no matter how impressive, would come down.

> ***Ezekiel 38:20*** And the fish of the sea, the birds of the heavens, the beasts of the field, all the creeping things that creep on the earth, and all the men who are on the face of the earth will shake at My presence; the mountains also will be thrown down, the steep pathways will collapse, **and every wall will fall to the ground.**

So Jesus begins to unfold the events that constitute the "birth pangs" — the process of labor that will issue in the full delivery of God's wrath upon mankind.

> ***Matthew 24:4*** And Jesus answered and said to them, 'See to it that no one misleads you.'

This should be our vital concern, for Jesus mentions it time and time again.

> ***Matthew 24:5*** 'For many will come in My name, saying, 'I am the Christ,' and will mislead many.'

What is a false christ or messiah? Could it be anyone who promises peace? Could it be those who promise that they have the solution to man's ills and that by believing in them and their political philosophy a country's problem with sin can be arrested and done away with? Does that sound like any politicians you know? Any heads of state? The reality is any organization that promotes man as the sole arbitrator by which peace is negotiated is fooling itself.

> ***Psalm 2:1*** Why are the nations in an uproar, And the peoples devising a vain thing? *2* The kings of the earth take their stand, And the rulers take counsel together Against the LORD and against His Anointed: *3* "Let us tear their fetters apart, And cast away their cords from us!"

Mankind continues to spawn this megalomania as delegates and high paid officials continue to delude themselves into thinking they are instruments of world peace when in reality they are but mere men, totally incapable of preventing the hand of Almighty God from descending and bringing judgment on mankind's sordid affairs. However good their intentions, all their efforts will soon be toppled as God brings judgment down on the blind and arrogant attitudes of world leaders around the globe.[30]

The Birth Pangs

For centuries, man has been pursuing the "golden ring" of wealth and acclaim, yet soon he will find out the futile struggle to find happiness and utopia outside of God's will simply cannot be. The road to peace stops at Jesus Christ, and all detractors of that cause, false messiahs — whether they are governments or individuals — will be laid to rest in the fast approaching millennium.

A plethora of false christs, evidenced by men rising in ascendancy and calling for global cooperation through the United Nations and NATO and myriads of other fractional organizations promoting global unity and peace, can all be looked on as representative of false christs as seen in

Revelation chapter 6 when Christ opens what is referred to as the first "seal."[31]

> ***Revelation 6:1*** And I saw when the Lamb broke one of the seven seals, and I heard one of the four living creatures saying as with a voice of thunder, 'Come.' ***2*** And I looked, and behold, a white horse, and he who sat on it had a bow; and a crown was given to him; and he went out conquering, and to conquer.

The "seals" Christ opens in the book of Revelation correspond perfectly in both content and order to the events He told the disciples would preclude His coming again as recorded in the Gospel of Matthew and Luke.

The first seal in Revelation depicts a false savior riding on a white horse equipped with a bow but without an arrow. Even without his weapon of war it says he went forth conquering and to conquer. Interpretations are legion concerning what this could mean, yet if we utilize Christ's insights as to what the first birth pang is in Matthew 24, we can see that He is referring to the appearance of false messiahs, men who endeavor to draw people away from following the true Prince of peace, Jesus Christ. Given that truth, this conquering could be referring to a conquering of the minds of the people of the world; people or leaders lulling others into the false assurance that by following them and not repenting or living under the lordship of Jesus Christ, the world can still achieve the goal of world peace outside of obedience to God. This is stunningly depicted by the well-attended conference which was held September 27th, 1995 and sponsored by the Gorbachev Foundation called, *"Toward a New Civilization: Launching a Global Initiative."* This conference, attended by 400-plus eminent personalities from fifty countries included such well-known leaders as former Secretary of State James Baker and George Shultz, former President George H.W. Bush, and former Prime Minister Margaret Thatcher. Additional participants were a virtual who's who of billionaires, presidents and vice presidents of countries along with a significant showing of Hollywood and media celebrities. Mr. Gorbachev opened the conference with this humble proposal:

> From the outset I would like to suggest that we consider the establishment of a global Brain Trust to focus on the present

and future of our civilization...because the main reason why we are lagging behind events, why we are mostly improvising and vacillating in the face of new developments, is that we are lagging behind in the thinking and rethinking of this new world. Of course, this idea of a Brain Trust can only succeed if endorsed and actively pursued by people who are widely respected as world leaders and global citizens.[32]

Does it sound like they plan on including you? Mr. Gorbachev seems to think that those who are the elite can get together and solve all the problems that plague mankind. At this conference of the elite our country's leaders mingled with such participants as Barbara Max Hubbard, author of *The Book of Co-Creation*. To get a feel for her philosophy and those she feels led to associate with, she writes in her book:

> Out of the full spectrum of human personality, one-fourth is electing to transcend...One-fourth is destructive [and] they are destructive seeds. In the past they were permitted to die a 'natural death.'... Now as we approach the quantum shift from the creature-human who is an inheritor of god-like powers - the destructive one-fourth must be eliminated from the social body... Fortunately, you are not responsible for this act. We are. We are in charge of God's selection process for planet Earth. He selects, we destroy. We are the riders of the pale horse, Death.

The startling truth is that Christ's words in Matthew 24 and the book of Revelation are happening now, and that leaders are preparing themselves to fulfill the vile and sickening tasks of the future.

> ***Matthew 24:6*** And you will be hearing of wars and rumors of wars; see that you are not frightened, for [those things] must take place, but [that] is not yet the end. *7* For nation will rise against nation, and kingdom against kingdom, and in various places there will be famines and earthquakes.

Certainly today we see the reality of wars and rumors of wars taking place. Anyone who lives outside the United States in less developed or communist countries knows full well the reality of wars and rumors of wars. The word "nation" here is the word *ethnos* and means "race, nation or people group." This type of ethnic conflict was fully exposed when the United States intervened in Bosnia. We have been witnesses to massacres in Rwanda by way of television and we have seen the bitter battle that took place in Chechnya as a proud people chose to defy submitting to the fractured Russian state. South Africa, with all its festering tribal conflicts, continues to be a raging sinkhole of misery and hatred. Man's bitterness and strife toward one another continues to rise unabated.

The word "kingdom" seen in verse 6 of Matthew is the word *basileia* and is used for spiritual kingdoms. This explains why we are seeing a growing animosity against Bible-believing Christians and those anywhere near their left or right. The United States is now moving to where the rest of the world has already been for some time — having a basic distrust and malevolence toward those preaching the unadulterated Word of God — a profound indicator that Satan has been hard at work swaying the core belief system that at one time held our nation.

Revelation 6:3-4 speaks about this glut of war by mankind when the second seal is opened. A red horse appears with a rider sitting on it that is given power to take peace from the face of the earth... *"that [men] should slay one another; and a great sword was given to him."* The Scripture states that power was *given* to the rider of the red horse, telling us that the rise in conflicts we see globally throughout the world is spiritually driven — preparing mankind to be drawn into the false promises of peace through the creation of world government.

A common rebuttal to this assertion is, "There have always been wars and rumors of war, how can you say that the time we're living in has anything to do with the end times?" The reason is because never before has peace been pursued in the Middle East like it is today, which is a critical and all important prerequisite for the return of Christ. Never before has the US held such a position of prominence and entrenched entanglement in every trouble spot around the world and never before have the institutions of "peace" and the false christs of paganism and materialism been so rampant. The allegiance of men to the sovereign God of the Bible who hold leadership positions in this country has been reduced to a mere whimper. Our nation is gasping for whatever spiritual principles it has left, and it is coming up empty, drowning and suffocating in a vacuum of greed and selfishness. It was this same wealth and insatiable appetite for sin that caused God to destroy Sodom and

Gomorrah, and will cause the downfall of the United States of America as well.[33]

> ***Ezekiel 16:49*** Behold, this was the guilt of your sister Sodom: she and her daughters had arrogance, abundant food, and careless ease, but she did not help the poor and needy. ***50*** Thus they were haughty and committed abominations before Me. Therefore I removed them when I saw [it.]

Yes, our nation stands guilty and the second seal will be opened. What then lies ahead?

> ***Matthew 24:7*** For nation will rise against nation, and kingdom against kingdom, and in various places there will be famines and earthquakes.

Even now we are beginning to see the tremors of this seal. When birth pangs of the prior two seals fully engage, this third pronouncement of Christ will show its face by way of famines, pestilences and earthquakes happening more than ever before.

The famines that occurred in Somalia, accompanied by the ravages of cholera and dysentery are but a preview of what is about to take place for the Bible says the effects of such plagues will affect a quarter of the earth as described in the opening of the fourth seal.[34] To verify the rapidity of earthquakes we have yet to experience, look how God has been slowly working up to the boiling point of what the world will experience during the full brunt of the Seventieth Week of Daniel.

During the thirty-eight year period from 1901 to 1938, there were 53 earthquakes that registered 6.99 or greater in magnitude. During the next thirty-eight years from 1939 to 1976 there were 71, and from 1977 to 2008 there have been 134, with 180 predicted by 2014 which would mark the end of that thirty-eight year period. Surely something is brewing. These figures from the US Geological Survey in Boulder, Colorado serve as indicators, warning bells, for those Christians who have eyes to see and ears to hear. They are meant to be spotlights to God's people that the times of the end are drawing nigh.

Jesus Christ, speaking from heaven in the book of Revelation gives us a clue as to what will precede the famine and pestilence of the scale just spoken of.

Revelation 6:5 And when He broke the third seal, I heard the third living creature saying, 'Come.' And I looked, and behold, a black horse; and he who sat on it had a pair of scales in his hand. ***6*** And I heard as it were a voice in the center of the four living creatures saying, 'A quart of wheat for a denarius, and three quarts of barley for a denarius; and do not harm the oil and the wine.'

The denarius was a unit of exchange in biblical times equivalent to a day's wage. A measure of wheat or three measures of barley were looked on as enough food to feed someone for a day and according to Scripture would require an entire day's wage to purchase. What can this mean?

It can either mean that in times to come food will be so scarce and the economy so bad that prices will be driven to this heightened level due to frenzied demand, or it could be referring to a monetary system that has gone out of control and is in the throes of hyper-inflation. This nightmare of fiscal insanity occurs when a country's currency loses its value every day, even every hour, as governments print worthless money in order to pay off their staggering and uncontrollable debt. It has happened before in many countries, and is happening in Zimbabwe even today as inflation is raging out of control. Argentina went down this road experiencing social chaos and 2000% inflation, and there is the lesson of Germany when during World War I the money became so debased through the non-stop printing of government money that a person needed a wheelbarrow full of dollars just to buy a loaf of bread.[35]

Does this tell us something about today? It tells us that this third seal could be the foretelling of an economic crash of such magnitude that it will throw the whole world into economic turmoil. In Western nations, the debt load that Satan has successfully tricked people into shouldering will come crashing down on them as the money markets they have stuffed their savings into will simply smolder in ruin. Man's obsession with accumulating wealth will be dealt a resounding blow as virtually everybody becomes a pauper overnight. Except a few. The Bible says to the angel of the third seal, "Hurt not the oil and the wine."

Oil and wine were looked on as items of wealth and abundance and here the angels were for some reason directed not to harm the oil and the wine. Could it be that this represents God holding in abeyance His judgment over the "the great men of the earth," those men who control

REVELATION UNRAVELED

seats of power and influence who capitalized and made millions on the misfortune of others in the crash of 1929?[36] By being privy to insider knowledge about the behavior of the Federal Reserve, they will be ready for the coming crash and will once again be waiting in the wings with ready cash, eager to buy up the ash heap of companies whose stock is a quarter or tenth of what it was worth just days before the great crash occurs. Many of these chief financiers, representing the world's most powerful men, will come out of this debacle richer and even more powerful so as to carry out their ultimate aim which is to use their wealth and influence to rule and bring in subjection the governments and the economies of the world into a "new world order."

> ***Revelation 6:7*** And when He broke the fourth seal, I heard the voice of the fourth living creature saying, 'Come.' ***8*** And I looked, and behold, an ashen horse; and he who sat on it had the name Death; and Hades was following with him. And authority was given to them over a fourth of the earth, to kill with sword and with famine and with pestilence and by the wild beasts of the earth.

This fourth seal describes a pale horse and he that sat on him was called Death and Hell followed Him. What a powerful and deadly seal this proves to be. The word "pale" comes from the word *chloros* which refers to a yellowish-green color, which gives humans a livid, plague stricken appearance. At the opening of this fourth seal, there will be unleashed in the world a vast array of death producing illnesses known as pestilence. Such pestilences reared their ugly heads when thousands of people died from cholera and dysentery as they fled from the country of Rwanda. The plague of AIDS has ravaged the continents of the world with an estimated 20 million dying of the disease between 1981 and the end of 2003. The numbers don't get all that better as time goes on with close to 36 million men and women living with the HIV/AIDS virus in 2007 and over two million dying of AIDS every year. These types of diseases will certainly all be prevalent during the fourth seal, but given the size and devastation the Bible talks about, it seems to indicate that weapons of mass destruction will also be unleashed to some degree by forces whose goal is clearly to bring the nations of the world to their knees through chaos and unbridled fear. Marvin J. Cetron, founder of Forecasting International Inc., whose organization warned the Department of Defense in 1994 of the exact scenario committed by

A Comparison of the Words of Christ

terrorists on September 11, 2001, predicts that further attacks on the scale of 9/11 are to be expected in France, Britain, and the United States over the next five to ten years.

There would be no better way to herd the masses of the unknowing public into the dissolution of our freedoms than by claiming a national emergency in order to implement the protective "remedies" waiting to be enacted by an all protective Federal government. How would this be accomplished? In ways you may not even be aware.

Government by Emergency

(FEMA), which stands for the Federal Emergency Management Agency has been given responsibility to carry out ALL executive orders if and when the President of the United States declares a national emergency, which can be initiated either by increased international tension, economic or environmental crisis. Under Executive Order 11051, the head of FEMA, not the President, has the authorization to implement 10 other executive orders. They are as follows:

Executive Order 10995 provides for the takeover of the communications media.

Executive Order 10997 provides for the takeover of all electric, power, petroleum, gas, fuels, and minerals.

Executive Order 10988 provides for the takeover of food resources and farms.

Executive Order 10999 provides for the takeover of all modes of transportation, control of highways, seaports, etc.

Executive Order 11000 provides for mobilization of all civilians into work brigades under the Government supervision.

Executive Order 11001 provides for Governmental takeover of all health, education and welfare functions.

Executive Order 11002 designates the Postmaster General to operate a national registration of all persons.

Executive Order 1103 provides for the Government to take over airports and aircraft.

Executive Order 1104 provides for the Housing and Finance Authority to relocate communities, designate areas to be abandoned, and establish new locations for populations.

Executive Order 1105 provides for the Government to take over railroads, inland waterways and public storage facilities.

All these executive orders were combined into Executive Order 11490 and were signed by President Carter on July 20, 1979, and are now law.[37]

When economic catastrophe hits our cities through an economic crash or environmental catastrophe, the 1993 Los Angeles riots will be looked on as a playground brawl compared to the real rebellion and anarchy that will begin to reign throughout our cities. Desperate and angry mobs will lash out and take what they need from store owners, powerless because of an exasperated and understaffed police force. Shock wave after shockwave of resultant woes will hit the TV screen through the news media — all adding fuel to the bonfire of social upheaval and distress that will be taking over our country and the world. This carefully crafted shock level of paranoia will purposefully glide the President into declaring a state of emergency and the initiation of the Presidential Executive Orders already signed into law. These executive orders will enable the President to circumvent the Constitution and the need for Congressional approval. World government at the hands of the beast would be on the horizon for the purpose of peace and security.

This type of governmental takeover by an all too eager President would set the stage for Operation Dragnet — implemented under the McCarron Act - Title II. At this stage of martial law, it is very possible US government officials will arrest all those men and women who have spoken out over the coming New World Order, namely militia groups, right-wing Christians, and those dedicated and outspoken patriots who make a point of warning their fellow citizens about the dangers of an overzealous government.[38]

The military, trained even as we speak in the confiscation and forfeiture of weapons from US citizenry, will be called on to disarm Americans for the sake of social order — an idea that has been nurtured and promoted through the mainstream press for the past few years.[39]

So it will be that through economic upheaval, the world will be catapulted into a governmental takeover and the America we once knew and loved will be only a memory. Poor countries will grow poorer still and suffer even greater hunger and hardship as the moral code of more developed nations begins to fray and break. Those killed with the sword mentioned in the fourth seal will undoubtedly come from the many that will be murdered and maimed during the coming moral meltdown along with those "enemies of the state" who are seen as obstacles to the establishment of governmental dictatorship.

Death by beasts of the earth in the fourth seal could come in a literal sense as ravenous animals begin to make man their prey, but could also refer to an epidemic of rabies and diseases of animals transferring over and smiting man as has been happening recently to the bewilderment of doctors. Doctors are now encountering strains of diseases never seen by modern man. These are the birth pangs, a sign from God of the impending birth of His judgment, for Jesus Christ opens these seals and the riders were given the power to carry out their loathsome deeds. These seals are God's messengers, sent to elicit repentance from all those who have eyes to see and ears to hear so they can escape the full force and fury of Satan's wrath to come as revealed and spoken of in the fifth seal, the Great Tribulation.

Verse 9 of Matthew 24 lays out the next chain of events to take place after the initial surge of these birth pangs.

> *Matthew 24:9* Then they will deliver you to tribulation, and will kill you, and you will be hated by all nations on account of My name. *10* And at that time many will fall away and will deliver up one another and hate one another. *11* And many false prophets will arise, and will mislead many.

The conditions will be ripe for such a defection of Christians to occur throughout the world and in the United States especially because the Christian faith has been so compromised and watered down there remains little of the true gospel left. Political correctness, the onslaught of feminism, and the butchering of the Word of God by most seminaries today have left spiritual leaders incapable of giving people the real answers they yearn for. Instead, accommodation, tolerance, and the compromising of all biblical principles for the sake of worldly acceptance has left much of the Christian church an empty shell and many ministers are to blame. They have left their first love and followed after idols — idols of stone, of brick, and buildings in which God does not dwell. They have concentrated on drawing others in by promoting the esoteric and self-love ideology of the 90s instead of placing a premium on dying to oneself and giving one's life in service to Jesus Christ the Lord. It is a papier-mâché Christianity. One that looks solid from the outside but is in reality paper-thin in strength and stability.

This papier-mâché faith, neither tested nor tempered by the Word of God, will crumble and fall with the onslaught of the fourth and fifth seal. Ministers, having fed their congregations a sugar-coated end times theology that the body of Christ will not even be on earth when any of the seals are seen, will soon find their faith beginning to crumble as seeds of bitterness toward supposed "men of the cloth" are sown among congregation members and take root. These ministers will have no answers to give because they too will have been deceived, having chosen not to take the words of Christ at face value, but instead believe in a theology that is bankrupt and destitute of the truth.

It will be during these dark days of the fourth seal that persecution will begin to take place against stalwart, Bible-believing Christians — those who see and are aware that the judgment of God is coming. Truck loads of "Christians," those who attend church regularly merely to be seen, with little regard for the truth of the message, will turn their hearts against true believers and disassociate themselves from those who have such "radical views" as God's judgments lay ahead. False prophets within the church who care little or nothing about the accuracy of God's Word, will find themselves chastising and belittling true believers who are willing to risk all to take a stand; and as the sifting of the true measure of men and women's hearts takes place, it will become a time when "iniquity shall abound and the love of many shall grow cold." With Christian churches fractured, and lawlessness and bedlam prevailing in our cities, the atmosphere will turn into an "every man for himself" mind-set with the government making true believers and patriots out to be villains.

Government Takes the Lead

This type of character assassination and innuendo was perfectly evidenced by former President Clinton's rhetoric in the aftermath of the Oklahoma City bombing. Within hours of the tragedy the President vehemently spoke out against *all* "radical right-wing extremists," militia groups, and the supposed "hate speech" of those who listen to talk radio and harbor anti-government sentiments. This calculated diatribe was pounded through the airwaves despite the increasing evidence of a government cover-up and views by the nation's foremost experts in demolition that all does not add up in our government's version of how the bombing took place.[40] The whole verbal witch hunt that occurred is a mere foretaste of the lies and threats that will be spoken by top government officials when the hours of crisis descend. It will be at this time that every Christian will have to decide whether they are like the seed that was planted on a rock, that when persecution came it withered because it had no root, or will they be like the seed that was planted in good ground, that takes root and brings forth good fruit unto everlasting life.

The groundswell of persecution that will begin at the fourth seal will come into full manifestation at the fifth seal, at or near the time of the abomination of desolation — when the armies of the Arab nations, armed by Russia and covertly by the United States, will begin to surround Jerusalem to take it by force.

The Great Tribulation Begins

Three and one half years after Israel signs the "covenant with death" which promises Israel peace with the Palestinians and their Arab neighbors, the Arab world will make their move by attacking Israel; and the United States along with UN/Coalition forces situated in Jerusalem will fail to deliver on their promise to keep the peace. At this time Israel and the Christian world will come under the siege of antichrist and the Great Tribulation will be underway. This is what Christ spoke about when He said in verse 9:

> ***Matthew 24:9*** Then they will deliver you to tribulation, and will kill you, and you will be hated by all nations on account of My name.

What the book of Revelation says is in direct correlation to the timing of the persecution spoken of in Matthew 24:9.

> ***Revelation 6:9*** And when He broke the fifth seal, I saw underneath the altar the souls of those who had been slain because of the word of God, and because of the testimony which they had maintained;

The opening of the fifth seal shows the martyred saints of God underneath the altar asking *"How long, O Lord, holy and true, wilt Thou refrain from judging and avenging our blood on those who dwell on the earth?"* This is God's way of describing the beginning of the Great Tribulation. Who are these saints under the altar? They are the raptured saints of the New Testament who had been martyred in centuries past. They are raised at the same time the faithful church is rescued; at the outset of the Great Tribulation. This is pointed out in verse 11.

> ***Revelation 6:11*** And there was given to each of them a white robe; and they were told that they should rest for a little while longer *[during the 3 ½ years of the Great Tribulation]*, until [the number of] their fellow servants and their brethren *[unfaithful Israel and the unfaithful church]* who were to be killed even as they had been, should be completed also *[during the time of the Great Tribulation]*. (italicized words added)

The concept that the elect are rescued from the hand of the antichrist and is comprised of those anxiously awaiting Christ's return and the faithful elect of Israel is mentioned by Jesus in verse 22 of Matthew 24.

> ***Matthew 24:22*** And unless those days had been cut short, no life would have been saved; but for the sake of the elect those days shall be cut short.

Jesus goes on to state in the Gospel of Matthew the timing of the rapture in the tribulation period.

> ***Matthew 24:37*** For the coming of the Son of Man will be just like the days of Noah. *38* For as in those days which were before the flood they were eating and drinking, they were marrying and giving in marriage, until the day that Noah entered the ark, *39* and they did not understand until the flood came and took them all away; so shall the coming of the Son of Man be. *40* Then there shall be two men in the field; one will be taken, and one will be left. *41* Two women [will be] grinding at the mill; one will be taken, and one will be left. *42* Therefore be on the alert, for you do not know which day your Lord is coming. *43* But be sure of this, that if the head of the house had known at what time of the night the thief was coming, he would have been on the alert and would not have allowed his house to be broken into. *44* For

this reason you be ready too; for the Son of Man is coming at an hour when you do not think [He will.]

We see here that Christ cannot be referring to people being raptured at the end of the Great Tribulation because Christ makes it analogous to the days of Noah, a time in which everybody was unaware and oblivious to the looming flood. This confirms that Jesus' return will be a surprise. For it to be a surprise, the rapture has to take place at or near the beginning of the Great Tribulation, not at the end, for at the end of the Great Tribulation the entire world knows they are under the judgment of Almighty God.

We are told in Revelation 13:5-6 and Daniel 7:25 that the Great Tribulation will not be cut short, but will last for 1260 days, which is 3 ½ years, the entire last half of the Seventieth Week of Daniel. We are also told that the beast will *make war on the saints and overcome them,* and that whosoever will not worship the beast and his image will be killed (Rev. 13:15). When we compare these saints in Revelation 13 to what we already know happens to the saints who are found "watching," the saints who suffer this massive persecution must be referring to "unprepared" Christians who are left on earth after the rapture and will be killed for the cause of Christ. They will allow themselves to be martyred rather than take the mark of the beast in the hope that they attain that better resurrection, the resurrection of the just due to take place at the end of the Seventieth Week of Daniel.

During this tribulation period many false prophets will arise and deceive many and yet only those who endure unto the end will make up the *final* elect when Christ comes to gather repentant Israel and raise the just from the dead. (Rev. 3:5)

The Two Witnesses

Matthew 24:14 And this gospel of the kingdom shall be preached in the whole world for a witness to all the nations, and then the end shall come.

This verse has been used by virtually every well-meaning evangelist and Bible teacher to say that the church needs to evangelize the world before the end can come. Is this really what it is saying?

Jesus reveals in the book of Revelation that during this time of extreme persecution, He will give power unto two witnesses, and that *they* will proclaim the kingdom of God to the entire world for 1260 days - the exact time period of the Great Tribulation. To do this job, Christ gives the two witnesses extraordinary supernatural power, to the degree that no one will be able to kill them — in fact, they will kill anyone who dares try to squelch their message (Rev. 11:3-5). They will also have power to stop it from raining on the earth for 3 ½ years and bring to pass plagues on a global scale. All this is God's failsafe method of evangelizing mankind given the persecution that will be taking place on all who trust or believe on Christ. When these two witnesses boldly proclaim God's truth, unassailable by anything man can do to stop them, you can be sure that as the media covers their ministry through the miracle of satellite technology, everyone around the world will have the opportunity to hear the message of God's kingdom.

At the culmination of the Seventieth Week of Daniel we find another event taking place that will bring into fruition the final criteria before Christ returns in glory.

> ***Revelation 14:6*** And I saw another angel flying in midheaven, having an eternal gospel to preach to those who live on the earth, and to every nation and tribe and tongue and people;

God will cause many supernatural events to take place, including having His message heralded by angels in order to bring to pass His saying that the everlasting gospel will be preached to the entire world. We can see that God will cause the entire world to hear the gospel by His angels and will not limit its outreach solely on the efforts of man.

> ***Matthew 24:23*** Then if anyone says to you, 'Behold, here is the Christ,' or There [He is'], do not believe [him.] *24* For false Christs and false prophets will arise and will show great signs and wonders, so as to mislead, if possible, even the elect. *25* Behold, I have told you in advance. *26* If therefore they say to you, 'Behold, He is in the wilderness,' do not go forth, [or], 'Behold, He is in the inner rooms,' do not believe [them.] *27* For just as the lightning comes from the east, and flashes even to the west, so shall the coming of the Son of Man be.

Jesus urged His followers during this time not to be deceived and succumb to the wide array of false prophets and deceptive lies that will be fashioned to cause their death and to deny Him. Christ speaks of this time as so strong in false doctrines and wonders that even the elect may be mislead. What does this mean? It could mean that believers will be tempted to renege on their faith due to the seductive claims of the devil to take the mark of the beast so as to participate in the cashless economy during that time. These "believers," so weak and worn down spiritually, will not have the resolve to stay true to Christ and will be the ones Christ erases from the book of life. Elect at one point, but now deceived and compelled to live for the devil. Having not endured to the end, these individuals will no longer be saved. Their faith in Christ has ceased. The tribulation will have served its purpose — it will have separated the genuine from the counterfeit, and a whoring bride from one who is true to her bridegroom.

At the end of Satan's campaign of terror, all men's eyes will be drawn towards the skies as celestial events unheard of and unimagined in the hearts of men begin to take place.

> *Matthew 24:29* But immediately after the tribulation of those days the sun will be darkened, and the moon will not give its light, and the stars will fall from the sky, and the powers of the heavens will be shaken,

This spectacle in the sky is the same as when the sixth seal is opened in the book of Revelation.

> *Revelation 6:12* And I looked when He broke the sixth seal, and there was a great earthquake; and the sun became black as sackcloth [made] of hair, and the whole moon became like blood; *13* and the stars of the sky fell to the earth, as a fig tree casts its unripe figs when shaken by a great wind. *14* And the sky was split apart like a scroll when it is rolled up; and every mountain and island were moved out of their places.

What does the glory of this worldwide spectacle mean? It will be proof to all the world that the Day of the Lord has begun, that God's sovereign hand and will is about to shake the land like never before.

> *Revelation 6:15* And the kings of the earth and the great men and the commanders and the rich and the strong and every slave and free man, hid themselves in the caves and among the rocks of the mountains; *16* and they said to the mountains

and to the rocks, 'Fall on us and hide us from the presence of Him who sits on the throne, and from the wrath of the Lamb; *17* for the great day of their wrath has come; and who is able to stand?'

What happens next? A period of woe known as the trumpet judgments, which we will study next as we delve into chapters eight and nine of the book of Revelation.

By careful scrutiny, we have seen that Jesus spoke forth the same prophetic truths in the Gospels that He uttered while in His glorified state in the book of Revelation. This makes perfect sense for Jesus Christ is *"the same yesterday, today, and forever."* It is now imperative for us to take heed unto His words and live our lives accordingly.

Chapter 6

The Chronology of the End Times

We have seen from Scripture who the beast is and that the events of the end times revolve around the Seventieth Week of Daniel. Now we will go a step further and take a comprehensive look at the entire scenario of how God has the book of Revelation set up so we can better understand not only the Seventieth Week of Daniel, but what God has in store for us in eternity and how He will bring about His ultimate rule.

To accomplish this goal, there is a chart in the Appendix of this book entitled *A Chronology of the End Times*. It is my hope that after this chapter, you will be able to fully grasp from the chart the chronology of events that will take place in the very near future. Another chart, *End Times Chronology,* is also in the Appendix and contains a list of many of the same events along with the scriptural documentation beside it. These two guides should give any student of the Bible ample material in which to study and make one's own.

The Seventieth Week Begins

The *Chronology of the End Times* chart begins in the upper left hand corner on page 175. As stated previously in this book, I believe that the Seventieth Week of Daniel will begin when Israel signs on to a comprehensive peace agreement with the Palestinians and the Arab world and this agreement will be instigated and brokered by the United States as a sure and lasting promise of peace to the Middle East. Daniel 9:27 and Isaiah 28:15 tell us that Israel will make what is called "a covenant with death" with the beast and the "many" (Arab nations?) and that this covenant marks the beginning of the Seventieth Week of Daniel. After the signing of this agreement, the first and second seals of Revelation will take center stage, with a rise in false Messiahs evidenced by both men and governmental ideologies promoting themselves as man's sole hope for peace and stability. Scripture makes clear however that these hopes will be dashed as those who seek to destroy Israel will meet certain and utter destruction. Listen to what Daniel 9:27 says again to help crystallize what we will now cover on the chart.

> ***Daniel 9:27*** And he will make a firm covenant with the many for one week, but in the middle of the week he will put a stop to sacrifice and grain offering; and on the wing of abominations [will come] one who makes desolate, even until a complete destruction, one that is decreed, is poured out on the one who makes desolate.

The Third and Fourth Seal Occur

Some time prior to the midpoint of the Seventieth Week one can expect to see the evidence of the third and fourth seal being opened. The third seal, most likely an economic crash coupled with irregular weather patterns, will produce famine and tremendous financial hardship around the globe. This financial crash will also set the backdrop for increased government intervention in order to restore order to what will turn out to be chaos in our cities and streets. The fourth seal being opened will bring about more famine plus pestilence and disease (both man-made and natural), along with increased earthquakes to the point that one quarter of the earth's population will be affected.

As these woes begin to happen, life will be such that people will *still* not see these events as indicative of God's judgment and the book of Revelation coming to pass. The liberal press will merely report it, the environmentalists will blame the phenomena as a result of global warming and man trashing the earth's resources, and religious persecution will pick up as the government and "enlightened" New Agers will target many of the social ills that are happening on right-wing extremists and dangerous religious cults. Through deception and lies, these politically correct soldiers of the New World Order will successfully turn the tide of public opinion against conservative, Bible-believing Christians who at this time may be voicing their concerns about the times of the end. I believe the Anti-Terrorism Act of 1996 and the Patriot Act of 2001 are forerunners of what Daniel 7:25 is talking about.

> ***Daniel 7:25*** And he *[the beast]* will speak out against the Most High and wear down the saints of the Highest One, and he will intend to make alterations in times and in law; and

they *[the saints]* will be given into his hand for a time, times, and half a time. (italicized words added)

The laws contained in those two anti-terrorism bills will ultimately be used some time in the future to shut down and silence any groups in this country who make a point of speaking out against encroaching world government or the abuse of power now being used by many of our Federal agencies. The further erosion of our Constitutional rights contained within the legislation is, in my opinion, direct preparation by our government for the last 3 ½ years of the Great Tribulation.

The Abomination of Desolation is Seen

Now move to the right side of the chart and look at the events due to take place during the last half of the Seventieth Week, which is 1260 days long, the same as 3 ½ years. The last half of the Seventieth Week begins with the armies of the beast taking over the Temple Mount area, an event known as the abomination of desolation. This takeover by Gentile forces, spearheaded by the United States, will ultimately allow Arab nations to attack Israel that will result in the escape of God's elect, the 144,000 Jews, to the ancient ruins of Petra situated in the region of Edom. This escape to Petra is mentioned in Isaiah 16:1-4, where the land of Sela, meaning "the rock," is referring to Petra.

The Rescue of the Faithful

The time frame of the escape of the elect also includes the rescue of the faithful church by way of the rapture. Look at how Christ states it in Luke 17:26-35.

> ***Luke 17:26*** And just as it happened in the days of Noah, so it shall be also in the days of the Son of Man: *[the parousia, that period of time that is part of the Son of Man's coming]* ***27*** they were eating, they were drinking, they were marrying, they were being given in marriage, until the day that Noah entered the ark, and the flood came and destroyed them all. ***28*** It was the same as happened in the days of Lot: they were eating, they were drinking, they were buying, they were selling, they were planting, they were building; *[Christ is making the point here that life will still be perceived as normal at this time]* ***29*** but on the day that Lot went out from

Sodom it rained fire and brimstone from heaven and destroyed them all *[i.e. judgment began]*. *30* It will be just the same on the day that the Son of Man is revealed. *31* On that day, let not the one who is on the housetop and whose goods are in the house go down to take them away; and likewise let not the one who is in the field turn back, *[this admonition of Christ's is the same He gave to people who see the abomination of desolation standing in the holy place. It is occurring at the correct time, right before the Great Tribulation begins]* *32* Remember Lot's wife. *33* Whoever seeks to keep his life shall lose it, and whoever loses [his life] shall preserve it. *34* I tell you, on that night there will be two men in one bed; one will be taken, and the other will be left. *35* There will be two women grinding at the same place; one will be taken, and the other will be left. (italicized words added)

This instantaneous disappearance is the event that Daniel 12:1 and Revelation 3:10 talk about:

Daniel 12:1 Now at that time *[the abomination of desolation of Dan. 11:45]* Michael, the great prince who stands [guard] over the sons of your people, will arise. And there will be a time of distress such as never occurred since there was a nation until that time; and at that time your people, everyone who is found written in the book, will be rescued. *[Who are they? They are the 144,000 Jews who will be taken from wherever they are to Petra. Some may be supernaturally transported there given that they all might not be in Jerusalem.]* (italicized words added)

I am aware that this section of the Scripture is written to the Jews, but one can also see the faithful church raptured at the same time. Look at Revelation 3:10...

Revelation 3:10 Because you have kept the word of My perseverance *[speaking of the faithful church]*, I also will keep you from the hour of testing, *[the Great Tribulation]* that [hour] which is about to come upon the whole world, to test those who dwell upon the earth. (italicized words added)

Luke 21:36 But keep on the alert at all times, praying in order that you may have strength to escape all these things that are about to take place *[in the Great Tribulation]*, and to stand before the Son of Man. (italicized words added)

By God's grace and mercy, we escape all the things that will be taking place during the Great Tribulation by being raptured. The reason this is true is because the abomination of desolation *begins* the Great Tribulation which lasts 3 ½ years and that is what the 144,000 and the faithful church are said to be rescued from.

The Fifth Seal - The Great Tribulation

The Great Tribulation begins with the opening of the fifth seal in the book of Revelation and shows the raptured, martyred saints asking, *"How long, O Lord, holy and true, dost thou not judge and avenge our blood on them that dwell on the earth?"* God uses this question, asked by these particular raptured saints, to indicate the Great Tribulation begins at the 5th seal by saying:

Revelation 6:11 And there was given to each of them a white robe; and they were told that they should rest for a little while longer, *[i.e. 3 ½ years]* until [the number of] their fellow servants and their brethren who were to be killed even as they had been, should be completed also *[during the Great Tribulation]*. (italicized words added)

These raptured saints, who had been previously martyred in the past, were told to rest in heaven until the rest of their brethren, which includes the unfaithful church and unfaithful Israel, are killed during the severe testing of the Great Tribulation. The martyrs of the Great Tribulation will then be raised at the resurrection of the just at the end of the 3 ½ years, a time in which rewards will be given to *all* the saints at the judgment seat of Christ.

The raptured saints spoken of at the fifth seal and in Revelation 7:9 are *not* rewarded until the resurrection of the just, when all the saints are together in heaven. The saints who have to be martyred during the Great Tribulation are not seen in heaven until much later in Revelation 15:2 and Revelation 20:4-5 at the resurrection of the just, where they are specifically cited then as *"those who had not worshipped the beast, neither his image, neither had received his mark upon their foreheads, or in their hands."* We as God's faithful church will not be subject to that testing, because we will be raptured at the flash point of the Great Tribulation, the abomination of desolation. Listen to Luke 17:30 again...

> ***Luke 17:30*** It will be just the same on the day that the Son of Man is revealed. ***31*** On that day, let not the one who is on the housetop and whose goods are in the house go down to take them away; and likewise let not the one who is in the field turn back. ***34*** I tell you, on that night there will be two men in one bed; one will be taken, and the other will be left. ***35*** There will be two women grinding at the same place; one will be taken, and the other will be left. ***36*** (Two men will be in the field; one will be taken and the other will be left.) ***37*** And answering they said to Him, 'Where, Lord?' And He said to them, 'Where the body [is,] there also will the vultures be gathered.' *[After the rapture, the vultures will gather around those left on earth, due to what will take place during the Great Tribulation.]* (italicized words added)

This scenario also lines up with 2 Thessalonians 2:1-7 where it states that Christians will see the man of sin revealed at the Temple Mount, and *then* the restrainer, (the faithful church) is taken out of the midst. Also remember Revelation 7:14 when the Apostle John asked the angel who these people were rejoicing in heaven.

> ***Revelation 7:14*** And I said to him, 'My lord, you know.' And he said to me, 'These are the ones who come out of the great tribulation, and they have washed their robes and made them white in the blood of the Lamb, *[these people who come out of the Great Tribulation are the faithful born-again believers and are clothed identically as the raptured martyred saints seen at the 5th seal]*

Look at chapter 13, verse 5...

> ***Revelation 13:5*** And there was given to him *[the beast]* a mouth speaking arrogant words and blasphemies; and authority to act for forty-two months was given to him. ***6*** And he opened his mouth in blasphemies against God, to blaspheme His name and His tabernacle, [that is], those who dwell in heaven. (italicized words added)

Who are these individuals who dwell in heaven that the beast is going to be cursing? Is he blaspheming angels? No, he is going to be blaspheming those believers who have been raptured and escaped his grip as he starts destroying Christians and Jews during the next 42 months!

The unfaithful church who is left behind are those people who Christ makes numerous mention of throughout His parables as not watching, not ready for their master's return, and their challenge will be to become "overcomers" and make it through the fiery testing of the Great Tribulation. Christ specifically warned His church that this would be the consequence of their unbelief. People of this unfaithful church, left behind during the rapture, will be called upon to be faithful and true to Christ by not taking the mark of the beast because the Bible says anyone who takes the mark of the beast will be damned. When this totalitarian world government takes place, a definite denouncement of true Christian faith will be demanded for it is the *modus operandi* of oppressive regimes that they stamp out any resistance to dictatorship — a resistance that comes first and foremost from believers in the one true God. Those who do not have the strength to make that kind of stand for Christ are going to fall into the category of men spoken of in Matthew 10:33.

> *Matthew 10:33* But whoever shall deny Me before men, I will also deny him before My Father who is in heaven.

This truth is found even in the church epistles where Paul says to Timothy:

> *2 Timothy 2:11* It is a trustworthy statement: For if we died with Him, we shall also live with Him; *12* If we endure, we shall also reign with Him; **If we deny Him, He also will deny us;**

That is my purpose for declaring this message — so each and every person can realize what the Bible says lies ahead and for you to be aware of what Christ says is required. When we decide to make Jesus Christ Lord of our lives, we should strive to bring every area of our lives under His Lordship. Where we fall short of that mark, we need to repent of that unfaithfulness and disobedience so as to be counted part of the "Philadelphia" church, that faithful church which will be raptured and not tested or deceived.

The Two Witnesses

It is at the beginning of the Great Tribulation that God will also raise up two witnesses, two men who are going to boldly proclaim God's truth for 3 ½ years, and who God protects from being harmed. Look at Revelation 11:3-6.

> ***Revelation 11:3*** And I will grant [authority] to my two witnesses, and they will prophesy for twelve hundred and sixty days, clothed in sackcloth. *4* These are the two olive trees and the two lamp stands that stand before the Lord of the earth. *5* And if anyone desires to harm them, fire proceeds out of their mouth and devours their enemies; and if anyone would desire to harm them, in this manner he must be killed. *6* These have the power to shut up the sky, in order that rain may not fall during the days of their prophesying; and they have power over the waters to turn them into blood, and to smite the earth with every plague, as often as they desire.

These two witnesses are God's *guarantee* that His Word will be spoken forth throughout the tribulation period — because unlike all the other people who will be martyred for taking a stand for Christ, these two witnesses cannot be killed until God allows it, and that happens at the end of the 3 ½ years.

The Great Tribulation will serve as a means to refine, purge, and purify those people who at one time professed belief in Christ but were seduced and swayed by the course of this world so as they produced no fruit or real love for Christ. In essence, when the rapture takes place, they will realize that the Word of God they were only vaguely familiar with is true, and they will be forced to come to a decision, "Am I going to live and stand for the Christ of the Scriptures, or am I going to worship and bow down to the beast — the false Christ of man?"

Government Control through the Mark of the Beast

It will be during this time of terrible persecution and iron-fist rule of the beast that the mark of the beast identification system will be initiated to weed out those who have decided to give their allegiance to Christ. The social and economic pressure struggling families will experience at the hand of government will be intense. Family members will have to decide whether or not to renounce their beliefs in order to gain access to the cashless economy by taking the mark of the beast. This decision will cause tremendous splintering among families because of the success Satan has achieved at steadily eroding the moral and spiritual foundation of the home. Informing or squealing on family members will start occurring just as Jesus said in Matthew 10:21:

> **Matthew 10:21** And brother will deliver up brother to death, and a father [his] child; and children will rise up against parents, and cause them to be put to death.

During this time, deceptive lies, propaganda, and temptations throughout the controlled media will make it all the easier for people of the world to be deceived. Stunningly, 2 Thessalonians 2:9 says that God believes they are getting what they deserve.

> **2 Thessalonians 2:8** And then that lawless one will be revealed whom the Lord will slay with the breath of His mouth and bring to an end by the appearance of His coming; **9** [that is,] the one whose coming is in accord with the activity of Satan, with all power and signs and false wonders, **10** and with all the deception of wickedness for those who perish, because they did not receive the love of the truth so as to be saved. *11 And for this reason God will send upon them a deluding influence so that they might believe what is false,* **12** in order that they all may be judged who did not believe the truth, but took pleasure in wickedness. (emphasis added)

The people who find themselves in this situation will be there because they chose not to receive the love of the truth when it was made available to them previously — through the Word of God taught in churches, on radio, or in the printed pages of the Bible. Instead, they chose to have pleasure in unrighteousness. If they want the blessing of eternal life now, they are going to have to pay for it with their lives because the level of persecution in the world at this time will require it. Jesus had already given them warning through the letters to the churches, the signs preceding the tribulation by the first four seals, and the preached Word of God. He made it abundantly clear, that when you decide to make Him Lord, you are supposed to make Him LORD!

REVELATION UNRAVELED

The Sixth Seal - A Sign from Heaven

Sometime during the last 3 ½ years, it is not clear when, the Day of the Lord sign will appear, also known as the sixth seal. It is spoken of in Revelation 6:12.

> ***Revelation 6:12*** And I looked when He broke the sixth seal, and there was a great earthquake; and the sun became black as sackcloth [made] of hair, and the whole moon became like blood; *13* and the stars of the sky fell to the earth, as a fig tree casts its unripe figs when shaken by a great wind. *14* And the sky was split apart like a scroll when it is rolled up; and every mountain and island were moved out of their places. *15* And the kings of the earth and the great men and the commanders and the rich and the strong and every slave and free man, hid themselves in the caves and among the rocks of the mountains; *16* and they said to the mountains and to the rocks, 'Fall on us and hide us from the presence of Him who sits on the throne, and from the wrath of the Lamb; *17* for the great day of their wrath has come; and who is able to stand?'

This unmistakable celestial sign marks a turning point in God's ultimate program. Satan will still be afflicting the children of God, but now *God's* judgments and wrath are due to set in as well.

The Trumpet Judgments Begin

The seventh seal marks the beginning of the trumpet judgments, which are described in Revelation 8:6 through Revelation 11:15. Satan, who at this time has been persecuting the saints during the tribulation period, will be "throttled down" to an extent as God's punishments descend on the earth. The afflictions that occur during the trumpet judgments will not only punish Israel for their unbelief and iniquity, but all of mankind. At this time the 144,000 Jews, who are safely tucked away in Petra, will be "sealed on the foreheads" by God's angels in order to protect them from the ravages of the trumpet judgments and specifically the fifth trumpet which will inflict every person on the face of the earth for five months. (Rev. 7:1-4)

> ***Revelation 8:6*** And the seven angels who had the seven trumpets prepared themselves to sound them. *7* And the first

sounded, and there came hail and fire, mixed with blood, and they were thrown to the earth; and a third of the earth was burned up, and a third of the trees were burned up, and all the green grass was burned up.

People argue that this is the result of nuclear war taking place. We cannot absolutely know that, so let's just look at what the results of these judgments are, and leave the details to God.

Revelation 8:8 And the second angel sounded, and [something] like a great mountain burning with fire was thrown into the sea; and a third of the sea became blood; *9* and a third of the creatures, which were in the sea and had life, died; and a third of the ships were destroyed.

Again, one cannot know exactly what this "great mountain burning with fire" is that was thrown into the sea. One can speculate all they want as to what causes it, but we can see the results and they are cataclysmic.

Revelation 8:10 And the third angel sounded, and a great star fell from heaven, burning like a torch, and it fell on a third of the rivers and on the springs of waters; *11* and the name of the star is called Wormwood; and a third of the waters became wormwood; and many men died from the waters, because they were made bitter.

With a third of the earth's drinking water supply poisoned, major problems will surely begin to take place because water is more important than food for survival.

Revelation 8:12 And the fourth angel sounded, and a third of the sun and a third of the moon and a third of the stars were smitten, so that a third of them might be darkened and the day might not shine for a third of it, and the night in the same way.

Whether this phenomenon is caused by volcanic ash being swept around the world, or nuclear fallout, or God's supernatural hand is unclear. Whatever the cause, it is going to be an eerie time on planet Earth as the whole foundation of life as man knows it — sunrise, sunset, and nighttime — are altered.

Revelation 8:13 And I looked, and I heard an eagle flying in mid-heaven, saying with a loud voice, 'Woe, woe, woe, to those who dwell on the earth, because of the remaining blasts of the trumpet of the three angels who are about to sound!' ***9:1*** And the fifth angel sounded, and I saw a star from heaven which had fallen to the earth; and the key of the bottomless pit was given to him. ***2*** And he opened the bottomless pit; and smoke went up out of the pit, like the smoke of a great furnace; and the sun and the air were darkened by the smoke of the pit. ***3*** And out of the smoke came forth locusts upon the earth; and power was given them, as the scorpions of the earth have power. ***4*** And they were told that they should not hurt the grass of the earth, nor any green thing, nor any tree, but only the men who do not have the seal of God on their foreheads. ***5*** And they were not permitted to kill anyone, but to torment for five months; and their torment was like the torment of a scorpion when it stings a man. ***6*** And in those days men will seek death and will not find it; and they will long to die and death flees from them.

"Locusts" are going to be unleashed when the bottomless pit is opened. The bottomless pit is used in Scripture to speak of a place where evil spirits have been sent and banned over the centuries. It is likely this plague of "locusts" will be fueled by evil spirits into a malicious and hideous plague of some kind that will torment and afflict every person except those who have the mark of God on their foreheads, which are the 144,000 mentioned earlier in Revelation 7:3-4.

We read in verse five that these locusts have power to torment men for five months and that their sting was like a sting of a scorpion. One does not have to be stung by a scorpion to realize the severity of this plague in that verse six says people will seek to die because of it but will not be able to.

The description of these locusts is given in verses 7-11. Some prophecy scholars use these descriptions such as "breastplates of iron," and "wings that sound like chariots" to say that these locusts have to be helicopter gunships afflicting man. I prefer to believe it is some supernatural plague by God, because gunships would not just wound people, they would be very successful at *killing* them. Besides that, it also says it will torment everyone, except the 144,000 for five months. No fleet of helicopters, however skilled, is going to be able to afflict the entire human population for five months. One fares better to just believe the Word and be done with it. God knows how He will do it.

> **Revelation 9:13** And the sixth angel sounded, and I heard a voice from the four horns of the golden altar which is before God, *14* one saying to the sixth angel who had the trumpet, 'Release the four angels who are bound at the great river Euphrates.' *15* And the four angels, who had been prepared for the hour and day and month and year, were released, so that they might kill a third of mankind. *16* And the number of the armies of the horsemen was two hundred million; I heard the number of them.

Commentaries say this army of 200 million is the army of the Red Chinese coming down toward Israel to kill a third of mankind. If you want to believe that, it is your privilege but the description of this army in verses 17-19, is very similar to what is described in Joel 2:1-11.

> **Joel 2:1** Blow a trumpet in Zion, And sound an alarm on My holy mountain! Let all the inhabitants of the land tremble, For the day of the LORD is coming; Surely it is near, *2* A day of darkness and gloom, A day of clouds and thick darkness. As the dawn is spread over the mountains, [So] there is a great and mighty people; There has never been [anything] like it, Nor will there be again after it To the years of many generations. *3* A fire consumes before them, And behind them a flame bums. The land is like the garden of Eden before them, But a desolate wilderness behind them, And nothing at all escapes them. *4* Their appearance is like the appearance of horses; And like war horses, so they run. *5* With a noise as of chariots they leap on the tops of the mountains, Like the crackling of a flame of fire consuming the stubble, Like a mighty people arranged for battle. *6* Before them the people are in anguish; All faces turn pale. *7* They run like mighty men; They climb the wall like soldiers; And they each march in line, Nor do they deviate from their paths. *8* They do not crowd each other; They march everyone in his path. When they burst through the defenses,

> They do not break ranks. *9* They rush on the city, They run on the wall; They climb into the houses, They enter through the windows like a thief. *10* Before them the earth quakes, The heavens tremble, The sun and the moon grow dark, And the stars lose their brightness. *11* And the LORD utters His voice **before His army;** Surely His camp is very great, For strong is he who carries out His word. The day of the LORD is indeed great and very awesome, And who can endure it? (emphasis added)

I prefer to see this army of 200 million as a supernatural force sent by God to kill one-third of mankind.

Amazingly enough, after seeing and living through all these horrible plagues that the trumpet judgments produce, man still refuses to repent.

> ***Revelation 9:20*** And the rest of mankind, who were not killed by these plagues, did not repent of the works of their hands, so as not to worship demons, and the idols of gold and of silver and of brass and of stone and of wood, which can neither see nor hear nor walk; *21* and they did not repent of their murders nor of their sorceries nor of their immorality nor of their thefts.

This gives the Christian remarkable insight into just how dark and evil the world will be at this point. *Man,* not just the supposed antichrist, but *man* will still refuse to repent and give up his sorceries, his idols, and his immorality. Man's vileness and corruption will be totally laid bare at this time.

As you continue to look at the chart, you can see the block that details the trumpet judgments. The next block down starts with the seventh trumpet, which in turn begins the bowl judgments. Before we go on to discuss these bowl judgments, there are some very important events that take place between the sixth trumpet and the seventh trumpet.

The Times of the Gentiles Is Fulfilled

The first truth we need to know is that the Gentile armies are going to have dominion over the saints of God and the holy city for 42 months. This can found in Revelation 11:2.

> ***Revelation 11:2*** And leave out the court which is outside the temple, and do not measure it, for it has been given to the nations; and they will tread underfoot the holy city for forty-two months.

Israel is going to be plundered and persecuted during this time, being punished for their iniquity until the 42 months (which is 3 ½ years) is fulfilled. Jesus Christ puts it another way in the Gospel of Luke.

> ***Luke 21:24*** and they *[Israel]* will fall by the edge of the sword, and will be led captive into all the nations; and Jerusalem will be trampled underfoot by the Gentiles until the times of the Gentiles be fulfilled. (italicized words added)

When the time of the Gentiles is fulfilled, Israel will no longer be blind spiritually, but will repent and recognize Christ as their Messiah. We see this from the book of Romans,

> ***Romans 11:25*** For I do not want you, brethren, to be uninformed of this mystery, lest you be wise in your own estimation, that a partial hardening has happened to Israel **until the fullness of the Gentiles has come in**; *26* and thus all Israel will be saved; just as it is written, 'The Deliverer will come from Zion, He will remove ungodliness from Jacob.' (emphasis added)

According to Scripture, amazing things will be happening at the end of these 3 ½ years. Jesus Christ the Deliverer will come to Zion. Daniel 12:1-2 lists what other things will take place after the abomination of desolation and the tribulation period.

> ***Daniel 12:2*** And many of those who sleep in the dust of the ground will awake, these to everlasting life, but the others to disgrace [and] everlasting contempt. *3* And those who have insight will shine brightly like the brightness of the expanse of heaven, and those who lead the many to righteousness, like the stars forever and ever. *4* But as for you, Daniel, conceal these words and seal up the book until the end of time; many will go back and forth, and knowledge will increase. *5* Then I, Daniel, looked and behold, two others were standing, one on this bank of the river, and the other on

that bank of the river. *6* And one said to the man dressed in linen, who was above the waters of the river, 'How long [will it be] until the end of [these] wonders?'

What wonders is Daniel referring to? The wonders he had been told about; namely the time of great distress, which is the Great Tribulation, and the rescue of those in the book, which is the rescue of the 144,000, and also the resurrection of those who sleep in the dust of the ground which is the resurrection of the just.

> ***Daniel 12:7*** And I heard the man dressed in linen, who was above the waters of the river, as he raised his right hand and his left toward heaven, and swore by Him who lives forever that it would be for a time, times, and half [a time]; and as soon as they *[the beast]* finish shattering the power of the holy people, all these [events] will be completed. (italicized words added)

A time, times, and half a time we know to be 3 ½ years, so the Scripture is telling us it will be 3 ½ years from the beginning of the Great Tribulation until the resurrection of the just. This time frame coincides perfectly with what we find taking place in the book of Revelation.

In chapter eleven of the book of Revelation and from the chart we see that as the last 1260 days of the Seventieth Week draw to a close, the beast finally kills the two witnesses. These two witnesses, who lay dead in the streets of Jerusalem for 3 ½ days, are then raised to life just before the seventh trumpet sounds. This is an important point to understand because in Revelation 10:7 it says:

> ***Revelation 10:7*** but in the days of the voice of the seventh angel, when he is **about to sound,** then the mystery of God is finished, as He preached to His servants the prophets. (emphasis added)

What is this mystery of God that is finished before the seventh trumpet sounds? It is the all-encompassing plan God had for Israel and all those who believe. It is best described in Daniel 9:24:

> ***Daniel 9:24*** Seventy weeks have been decreed for your people and your holy city, to finish the transgression, to make an end of sin, to make atonement for iniquity, to bring

in everlasting righteousness, to seal up vision and prophecy, and to anoint the most holy [place.]

At the end of the Seventieth Week, Israel will have *finished their transgression* of forsaking God's protection and going into covenant with the beast in return for false security. They will have *made an end of sins* by realizing their mistake and their apostasy toward God by repenting and accepting Jesus Christ as their King and Messiah.[41] God will have made reconciliation and *atonement for their iniquity* through the thorough and awesome punishment they received at the hand of the beast and God's own hand through the trumpet judgments.[42] At this point in time God will also begin to *bring in everlasting righteousness* as He punishes Israel's enemies and begins to restore Jerusalem and the surrounding area for their everlasting possession and enjoyment.[43] At this point Israel will, as Isaiah 10:20 says, "never rely on the one who struck them *[referring to the beast],* but will truly rely on the LORD, the Holy One of Israel."

The Last Day / The Resurrection of the Just

Daniel 9:24 is fulfilled at the end of the Seventieth Week and it marks the fulfillment of God dealing with Israel and the believing saints on this present earth. Remember that the statement "those who sleep in the dust of the earth will awake" in Daniel 12:2 was also included in the wonders to be accomplished within the "time, times, and half a time." We go to the Gospel of John now to help us understand more about the timing of the resurrection of the just. Jesus Christ makes it very clear when it occurs.

> *John 6:39* And this is the will of Him who sent Me, that of all that He has given Me I lose nothing, but raise it up on **the last day.**
>
> *John 6:40* For this is the will of My Father, that everyone who beholds the Son and believes in Him, may have eternal life; and I Myself will raise him up on **the last day.**
>
> *John 6:44* No one can come to Me, unless the Father who sent Me draws him; and I will raise him up on **the last day.**
>
> *John 6:54* He who eats My flesh and drinks My blood has eternal life, and I will raise him up on **the last day.**

Jesus cannot be talking about raising the just on the last day of the bowl judgments which ends with the Battle of Armageddon because according to Revelation 15:1-3 the saints of God are already in heaven *before* those bowl judgments occur. This truth is plainly seen in Revelation 15:1-3.

> **Revelation 15:1** And I saw another sign in heaven, great and marvelous, seven angels who had seven plagues, [which are] the last, because in them the wrath of God is finished. *2* And I saw, as it were, a sea of glass mixed with fire, and those who had come off victorious from the beast and from his image and from the number of his name, standing on the sea of glass, holding harps of God. *[These people are the saints of the Great Tribulation who have been resurrected at the resurrection of the just; in that they were victorious in standing against the mark of the beast]* 3 And they sang the song of Moses the bond-servant of God and the song of the Lamb, saying, "Great and marvelous are Thy works, O Lord God, the Almighty; Righteous and true are Thy ways, Thou King of the nations. *5* After these things I looked, and the temple of the tabernacle of testimony in heaven was opened, *6* and the seven angels who had the seven plagues came out of the temple, clothed in linen, clean [and] bright, and girded around their breasts with golden girdles. *7* And one of the four living creatures gave to the seven angels seven golden bowls full of the wrath of God, who lives forever and ever. *8* And the temple was filled with smoke from the glory of God and from His power; and no one was able to enter the temple until the seven plagues of the seven angels were finished. (italicized words added)

Verses 2 and 3 of Revelation 15 establish that the martyred saints of the tribulation period, those who were faithful to Christ and did not take the mark of the beast, are in heaven BEFORE the angels depart to deliver the bowl judgments on unbelieving mankind. This means then that the resurrection of the just *must* take place before the bowl judgments and occur on the *last day* of the Seventieth Week of Daniel. This is exactly the case, for in Revelation 10:5-7 we see a "strong" seventh angel, who has many of the same characteristics of the Deliverer, Jesus Christ, come down from heaven on a cloud and declare that when he sounds, the mystery of God is complete. The similarities of the seventh angel to Jesus Christ are striking (Rev. 10:1-3; Rev. 1:14-16; and Ezek. 1:27-28). This heralding of the end by the seventh angel, aligns perfectly with this being the last day of the Seventieth Week of Daniel, the precise time that Christ said He would raise and gather unto Himself all those who believed on Him and it also coincides with the time that the two witnesses are resurrected from the streets of Jerusalem by "a voice from heaven." It all happens right before the seventh trumpet sounds — *the last day of the Seventieth Week of Daniel.*

We can see Christ beginning the harvest of the world at this time with the help of His angels by looking at Revelation 14:14.

> ***Revelation 14:14*** And I looked, and behold, a white cloud, and sitting on the cloud [was] one like a son of man having a golden crown on His head, and a sharp sickle in His hand. *15* And another angel came out of the temple, crying out with a loud voice to Him who sat on the cloud, "Put in your sickle and reap, because the hour to reap has come, because the harvest of the earth is ripe." *[This is all taking place before the bowl judgments begin]* *16* And He *[Jesus]* who sat on the cloud swung His sickle over the earth; and the earth was reaped. (italicized words added)

This record also lines up with Matthew 24:30 and with Ezekiel, chapter 37.

> ***Matthew 24:30*** and then the sign of the Son of Man will appear in the sky, and then all the tribes of the earth will mourn, and they will see the Son of Man coming on the clouds of the sky with power and great glory. *31* And He will send forth His angels with a great trumpet and they will gather together His elect from the four winds from one end of the sky to the other *[Again, this is before the Battle of Armageddon]*

During this harvest of the world, Jesus Christ will descend from heaven and will place His feet on the Mount of Olives and split it in half in order to provide an escape route for the repentant of Israel that are still alive, so they can be protected from the destruction ready to begin in the bowl judgments. This is spoken of by the prophet Zechariah.

> ***Zechariah 14:4*** And in that day His feet will stand on the Mount of Olives, which is in front of Jerusalem on the east; *[This is Christ coming down in a cloud as the angel in Acts 2:11 said He would]* and the Mount of Olives will be split in its middle from east to west by a very large valley, so that half of the mountain will move toward the north and the other half toward the south. *5* And you will flee by the valley of My mountains, *[speaking of repentant Israel who will flee from the destruction of the bowl judgments that are about to begin]* for the valley of the mountains will reach to Azel *[which is a secret, protective place]*; yes, you will flee just as you fled before the earthquake in the days of Uzziah king of Judah. Then the LORD, my God, will come, [and] all the holy ones with Him. *[This is talking about the raptured saints and those recently resurrected in the resurrection of the just when they come back with Christ later at the culmination of the bowl judgments — the Battle of Armageddon]* (italicized words added)

Isaiah speaks some more about the protection of repentant Israel that occurs at the resurrection of the just.

> ***Isaiah 26:19*** Your dead will live; Their corpses will rise. You who lie in the dust, awake and shout for joy, For your dew is as the dew of the dawn, And the earth will give birth to the departed spirits. *[When? At the resurrection of the just]* *20* Come, my people *[repentant Israel]*, enter into your rooms, *[at Azel],* And close your doors behind you; Hide for a little while, Until indignation *[the bowl judgments]* runs [its] course. *21* For behold, the LORD is about to come out from His place To punish the inhabitants of the earth for their iniquity; And the earth will reveal her bloodshed, And will no longer cover her slain. *[Those told to hide are most likely those of repentant Israel who flee to Azel because saints in heaven would not be referred to as "hiding"]* (italicized words added)

I also believe chapter 37 of Ezekiel describes the resurrection of the just. To me, this chapter is not merely describing the return of the Jewish people to the land of Israel through immigration in the last days, but instead gives a vivid depiction of what will take place as Christ and His angels go out to reap the earth.

> *Ezekiel 37:1* The hand of the LORD was upon me, and He brought me out by the Spirit of the LORD and set me down in the middle of the valley; and it was full of bones. *2* And He caused me to pass among them round about, and behold, [there were] very many on the surface of the valley; and lo, [they were] very dry. *3* And He said to me, 'Son of man, can these bones live?' And I answered, 'O Lord GOD, Thou knowest.' *4* Again He said to me, 'Prophesy over these bones, and say to them, 'O dry bones, hear the word of the LORD.' *5* 'Thus says the Lord GOD to these bones, 'Behold, I will cause breath to enter you that you may come to life. *6* 'And I will put sinews on you, make flesh grow back on you, cover you with skin, and put breath in you that you may come alive; and you will know that I am the LORD.' *[This is what God had the prophets do many times. He told them what to speak out so as to bring the promise of God into existence]* *7* So I prophesied as I was commanded; and as I prophesied, there was a noise, and behold, a rattling; and the bones came together, bone to its bone. *8* And I looked, and behold, sinews were on them, and flesh grew, and skin covered them; but there was no breath in them. *9* Then He said to me, 'Prophesy to the breath, prophesy, son of man, and say to the breath, 'Thus says the Lord GOD,' **Come from the four winds**, O breath, and breathe on these slain, that they come to life. *[This term, "from the four winds" is the same term used by Christ in Matt. 24:31 when He described how His angels will gather His elect from the four winds]* So I prophesied as He commanded me, and the breath came into them, and they came to life, and stood on their feet, an exceedingly great army. *[This army of resurrected Israel will, along with the rest of the saints in heaven, be the heavenly army that will return with Christ later in judgment against the armies of the world at the Battle of Armageddon].* Then He said to me, Son of man, these bones are the whole house of Israel; behold, they say, 'Our bones are dried up, and our hope has perished. We are completely

cut off *12* Therefore prophesy, and say to them, 'Thus says the Lord GOD, 'Behold, I will open your graves and cause you to come up out of your graves, My people; and I will bring you into the land of Israel. *13* Then you will know that I am the LORD, when I have opened your graves and caused you to come up out of your graves, My people. *14* And I will put My Spirit within you, and you will come to life, and I will place you on your own land. *[A promise that God will bring to pass in the Millennial kingdom]* Then you will know that I, the LORD, have spoken and done it, 'declares the LORD.' (italicized words added)

The Sheep and Goat Judgment

When this great gathering takes place, Jesus is going to do some separating in what is called the "sheep and goat judgment." It is a time when He is going to winnow from resurrected Israel and saints who have died in the past, those who did not really love or obey Him. To fully understand and accept this truth, we have to go to the 25th chapter of the Gospel of Matthew to see how the kingdom of heaven will come about according to Christ Himself. Verses 1 through 12 speak about the parable of the ten virgins and the importance of being prepared for the bridegroom when he arrives. Then Jesus says that the kingdom of heaven is also like a man who goes on a journey, and before leaving, entrusts his slaves with his possessions — referred to as talents, a gift amounting to around a thousand dollars per talent. Let's read the record in Matthew 25:15.

> *Matthew 25:15* And to one he gave five talents, to another, two, and to another, one, each according to his own ability; and he went on his journey. *16* Immediately the one who had received the five talents went and traded with them, and gained five more talents. *17* In the same manner the one who [had received] the two [talents] gained two more. *18* But he who received the one [talent] went away and dug in the ground, and hid his master's money. *[He did nothing with it]* *19* Now after a long time the master of those slaves came and settled accounts with them. *20* And the one who had received the five talents came up and brought five more talents, saying, 'Master, you entrusted five talents to me; see, I have

gained five more talents.' *21* His master said to him, 'Well done, good and faithful slave; you were faithful with a few things, I will put you in charge of many things, enter into the joy of your master.' *22* The one also who [had received] the two talents came up and said, 'Master, you entrusted to me two talents; see, I have gained two more talents.' *23* His master said to him, 'Well done, good and faithful slave; you were faithful with a few things, I will put you in charge of many things; enter into the joy of your master.' *24* And the one also who had received the one talent came up and said, 'Master, I knew you to be a hard man, reaping where you did not sow, and gathering where you scattered no [seed.] *[He actually started complaining to the master that he expected too much!]* *25* 'And I was afraid, and went away and hid your talent in the ground; see, you have what is yours.' *26* But his master answered and said to him, 'You wicked, lazy slave, you knew that I reap where I did not sow, and gather where I scattered no [seed.] *27* 'Then you ought to have put my money in the bank, and on my arrival I would have received my [money] back with interest, *[i.e. the master expected fruit!]* *28* 'Therefore take away the talent from him, and give it to the one who has the ten talents.' *29* For to everyone who has shall [more] be given, and he shall have an abundance; but from the one who does not have, even what he does have shall be taken away. *30* And cast out the worthless slave into the outer darkness; in that place there shall be weeping and gnashing of teeth. (italicized words added)

It is easy to see the parallels Jesus was making to Himself. Jesus was saying that upon His departure from earth, He would give "a talent," which could be construed here the Holy Spirit, accurately called in Scripture our "gift." When He returns, He expects to see that something was done with it for His benefit. What happens to the servant who has nothing to show for the gift? Christ will chastise the lazy servant, *take away* his "gift," in this case the Holy Spirit, and then sentence him to outer darkness where there will be weeping and gnashing of teeth. With that story being told, Christ goes right into describing the sheep and goat judgment in detail of what will take place at the resurrection of the just. All the same lessons apply.

Matthew 25:31 But when the Son of Man comes in His glory, and all the angels with Him, then He will sit on His glorious throne. *32* And all the nations *[ethnos; a company troop or swarm, multitude of individuals of the same nature or genus, Paul even used the word to refer to Gentile Christians]* will be gathered before Him; and He will separate them from one another, as the shepherd separates the sheep from the goats; *33* and He will put the sheep on His right, and the goats on the left. *34* Then the King will say to those on His right, 'Come, you who are blessed of My Father, inherit the kingdom prepared for you from the foundation of the world. *35* For I was hungry, and you gave Me [something] to eat; I was thirsty, and you gave Me drink; I was a stranger, and you invited Me in; *36* naked, and you clothed Me; I was sick, and you visited Me; I was in prison, and you came to Me.' *37* Then the righteous will answer Him, saying, 'Lord, when did we see You hungry, and feed You, or thirsty, and give You drink? *38* And when did we see You a stranger, and invite You in, or naked, and clothe You? *39* And when did we see You sick, or in prison, and come to You?' *40* And the King will answer and say to them, 'Truly I say to you, to the extent that you did it to one of these brothers of Mine, [even] the least [of them,] you did it to Me.' *[This is the epitome of living out Christ's command to love God and love your neighbor as yourself]* *41* Then He will also say to those on His left, 'Depart from Me, accursed ones, into the eternal fire which has been prepared for the devil and his angels; *42* for I was hungry, and you gave Me [nothing] to eat; I was thirsty, and you gave Me nothing to drink; *43* I was a stranger, and you did not invite Me in; naked, and you did not clothe Me; sick, and in prison, and you did not visit Me. *44* Then they themselves also will answer, saying, 'Lord, when did we see You hungry, or thirsty, or a stranger, or naked, or sick, or in prison, and did not take care of You?' *45* Then He will answer them, saying, **'Truly I say to you, to the extent that you did not do it to one of the least of these, you did not do it to Me.'** *[they were not doers of the Word but hearers only]* **46 And these** will go away into eternal punishment, but the righteous into eternal life. (italicized words and emphasis added)

This is exactly what happens according to Daniel 12:2 where it says *"many will wake from the dust of the earth to everlasting life and others to shame and everlasting contempt."* These "others" are those who at one time were followers of Jehovah, or followers of Christ, but failed to confess the Lord when tested, or chose not to practice the Word in their lives. To these people Christ will say, "Depart from me, ye that work iniquity." The reality of Christ separating the true sheep from the goats is the entire subject of Ezekiel 34, where the Lord condemns the spiritual leaders of Israel for not truly serving the needs of the people. Listen to the Lord's stunning rebuke:

> ***Ezekiel 34:2*** Son of man, prophesy against the shepherds of Israel. Prophesy and say to those shepherds, 'Thus says the Lord GOD, 'Woe, shepherds of Israel who have been feeding themselves! Should not the shepherds feed the flock? *3* You eat the fat and clothe yourselves with the wool, you slaughter the fat [sheep] without feeding the flock. *4* **Those who are sickly you have not strengthened, the diseased you have not healed, the broken you have not bound up, the scattered you have not brought back, nor have you sought for the lost; but with force and with severity you have dominated them...** *11* For thus says the Lord GOD, 'Behold, I Myself will search for My sheep and seek them out. *12* As a shepherd cares for his herd in the day when he is among his scattered sheep, so I will care for My sheep and will deliver them from all the places to which they were scattered on a cloudy and gloomy day...*[a reference to what it will be like at the end of the Seventieth Week of Daniel, see Zeph. 1:15]* *15* 'I will feed My flock and I will lead them to rest' declares the Lord GOD. *16* 'I will seek the lost, bring back the scattered, bind up the broken, and strengthen the sick; **but the fat and the strong I will destroy.** *[Who is He talking about? He is talking about the arrogant and selfish shepherds who did not serve the people as they should have!]* I will feed them with judgment...Behold, I will judge between one sheep and another, between the rams and the male goats.'

REVELATION UNRAVELED

This powerful chapter sets in vivid detail the reckoning God will have on reprobate and deceitful workers among His people. It will happen when the righteous judge, Jesus Christ, returns to gather His flock on the last day of the Seventieth Week of Daniel and it will be accomplished through the resurrection of the just and the sheep and goat judgment as set forth in Matthew 25:31-36. This truth is also clearly stated in Matthew 13, when Jesus gives the parable of the tares (weeds) which follows immediately after the famed "sower and the seed" parable where Christ explains that of all those who hear the Word of God only those planted on good ground will ultimately bring forth fruit. He begins the story of the tares in verse 24.

> *Matthew 13:24* He presented another parable to them, saying, 'The kingdom of heaven may be compared to a man who sowed good seed in his field. *25* But while men were sleeping, his enemy came and sowed tares also among the wheat, and went away. *26* But when the wheat sprang up and bore grain, then the tares became evident also. *27* And the slaves of the landowner came and said to him, 'Sir, did you not sow good seed in your field? How then does it have tares?' *28* And he said to them, 'An enemy has done this!'

Jesus says that amongst believers, the devil will sow "tares," which is a darnel, a weed that *resembles* wheat. An enemy sowed this corrupt strain within the field, just as the devil sows corrupt believers within the church. The slaves of the landowners then ask their master the question...

> *Matthew 13:28(b)* ... 'Do you want us, then, to go and gather them up?' *29* But he said, 'No; lest while you are gathering up the tares, you may root up the wheat with them. *30* Allow both to grow together until the harvest; and in the time of the harvest I will say to the reapers, 'First gather up the tares and bind them in bundles to burn them up; but gather the wheat into my barn.'

In order to protect the true wheat from being uprooted, Jesus says it is best to wait until the harvest and then the reapers will gather the tares to burn them (in the bowl judgments), but the wheat (true believers) will be gathered into his barn (heaven). He says this when He explains the parable to His disciples in verse 36.

Matthew 13:36 And His disciples came to Him, saying, 'Explain to us the parable of the tares of the field.' *37* And He answered and said, 'The one who sows the good seed is the Son of Man, *38* and the field is the world; and [as for] the good seed, these are the sons of the kingdom; and the tares are the sons of the evil [one]; *39* and the enemy who sowed them is the devil, and the harvest is the end of the age; and the reapers are angels. *40* Therefore just as the tares are gathered up and burned with fire, so shall it be at the end of the age. *41* The Son of Man will send forth His angels, *[this occurs at the resurrection of the just when Christ returns with His angels to harvest the world before the horrible bowl judgments take place]*[44] and they will gather out of His kingdom all stumbling blocks, and those who commit lawlessness, *[the corrupt within the church — I Jn. 3:4,6]* *42* and will cast them into the furnace of fire; in that place there shall be weeping and gnashing of teeth. *43* Then the righteous will shine forth as the sun in the kingdom of their Father. He who has ears, let him hear. (italicized words added)

This puts a classic chapter in the Gospels in perfect perspective. Listen to what Christ says about the Pharisees in Matthew 23...

Matthew 23:2 The scribes and the Pharisees have seated themselves in the chair of Moses; *3* therefore all that they tell you, do and observe, but do not do according to their deeds; for they say [things,] and do not do [them.]

Jesus is saying here that the Pharisees are hypocrites; they say one thing but do another. He warns His disciples not to emulate them. He continues by saying...

Matthew 23:4 And they tie up heavy loads, and lay them on men's shoulders; but they themselves are unwilling to move them with [so much as] a finger. *5* But they do all their deeds to be noticed by men; for they broaden their phylacteries, and lengthen the tassels [of their garments.] *6* And they love the place of honor at banquets, and the chief seats in the synagogues, *7* and respectful greetings in the market places, and being called by men, Rabbi. *8* But do not be called

Rabbi; for One is your Teacher, and you are all brothers. *9* And do not call [anyone] on earth your father; for One is your Father, He who is in heaven. *10* And do not be called leaders; for One is your Leader, [that is,] Christ. *11* But the greatest among you shall be your servant... *25* Woe to you, scribes and Pharisees, hypocrites! For you clean the outside of the cup and of the dish, but inside they are full of robbery and self-indulgence. *26* You blind Pharisee, first clean the inside of the cup and of the dish, so that the outside of it may become clean also *27* Woe to you, scribes and Pharisees, hypocrites! **For you are like whitewashed tombs which on the outside appear beautiful, but inside they are full of dead men's bones and all uncleanness. *28* Even so you too outwardly appear righteous to men, but inwardly you are full of hypocrisy and lawlessness.** *[What judgment does Christ pronounce upon them?]* *33* You serpents, you brood of vipers, **how shall you escape the sentence of hell?** (italicized words and emphasis added)

Christ did not mind offending these wayward Jewish rabbis. He told it like it was, saying that if they did not start living what the Word of God said, they would be sentenced to hell. This tells us that people who know the Scriptures, but choose to reject them and instead live hypocritical lives are going to suffer consequences — all of which Christ spoke about plainly in the parables. The truth, plain and simple is that the true sheep, followers of Jesus Christ, are going to be separated from the counterfeits — the goats. We can see this directly in the Gospel of Matthew, chapter 8, verses 11-12.

Matthew 8:11 And I say to you, that many shall come from east and west, and recline [at the table] with Abraham, and Isaac, and Jacob, in the kingdom of heaven; *[at the resurrection of the just]* *12* but the sons of the kingdom shall be cast out *["cast out" is the Greek word ekballo in the KJV, it means "to banish from a family, to bid one to depart"]* into the outer darkness; in that place there shall be weeping and gnashing of teeth. (italicized words added)

The context of this verse is when Christ singled out the genuine faith of the Gentile centurion when the centurion asked Jesus to heal his servant. Jesus made the point to all those surrounding Him that many in Israel will be surprised when they see Abraham and Isaac sitting down to the wedding feast, but many of those in Israel who are sons of the kingdom through heritage, will be cast into outer darkness because of their unbelief.

The importance of having true faith in Christ and acting on His Word with a pure heart is set forth by Jesus in Matthew 7...

> *Matthew 7:18* A good tree cannot produce bad fruit, nor can a bad tree produce good fruit. *19* Every tree that does not bear good fruit is cut down and thrown into the fire. *20* So then, you will know them by their fruits. *21* Not everyone who says to Me, 'Lord, Lord,' will enter the kingdom of heaven; but he who does the will of My Father who is in heaven. *22* Many will say to Me on that day, 'Lord, Lord, did we not prophesy in Your name, and in Your name cast out demons, and in Your name perform **many** miracles?' *[These were not your run of the mill unbelievers — they were Christians!]* *23* And then I will declare to them, 'I never knew you; depart from Me, you who practice lawlessness.' *[These are the people who are gathered by the angels to be burned in Matt. 13:41]* *24* Therefore everyone who hears these words of Mine, and acts upon them, may be compared to a wise man, who built his house upon the rock. *25* And the rain descended, and the floods came, and the winds blew, and burst against that house; and [yet] it did not fall, for it had been founded upon the rock. *26* And everyone who hears these words of Mine, and does not act upon them *[i.e. practices lawlessness],* will be like a foolish man, who built his house upon the sand. *27* And the rain descended, and the floods came, and the winds blew, and burst against that house; and it fell, and great was its fall.

There are a few other people you might recognize who will be classified as a goat. Look at Matthew 10:32...

> *Matthew 10:32* Everyone therefore who shall confess Me before men, I will also confess him before My Father who is in heaven. *33* But whoever shall deny Me before men, I will also deny him before My Father who is in heaven.

Do you believe what Jesus Christ says? We can hear Him state this principle first hand when speaking about some leaders in John 12:42...

> *John 12:42* Nevertheless many even of the rulers believed in Him, but because of the Pharisees they were not confessing [Him], lest they should be put out of the synagogue; *43* for they loved the approval of men rather than the approval of God. *[This kind of compromising on behalf of powerful men or what people will say about you was as prevalent back then as it is today. What does Jesus Christ say about these types of people?]* *44* And Jesus cried out and said, "He who believes in Me does not believe in Me, but in Him who sent Me. *45* And he who beholds Me beholds the One who sent Me. *46* I have come [as] light into the world, that everyone who believes in Me may not remain in darkness. *47* And if anyone hears My sayings, and does not keep them, I do not judge him; for I did not come to judge the world, but to save the world. *48* He who rejects Me, and does not receive My sayings, has one who judges him; **the word I spoke is what will judge him at the last day.** (italicized words and emphasis added)

Jesus said in Matthew 10:32 that *"whoever denies me before men I will deny him before my Father in heaven."* We must realize then that these words of Christ will be used to judge every person who fails to take a stand for Him when worldwide tyranny prevails.

The importance of abiding and staying in fellowship with Christ is everything. It is spoken about by Christ in John 15...

> *John 15:1* I am the true vine, and My Father is the vinedresser. *2* Every branch in Me that does not bear fruit, He takes away; and every [branch] that bears fruit, He prunes it, that it may bear more fruit. *3* You are already clean because of the word which I have spoken to you. *4* Abide in Me, and I in you. As the branch cannot bear fruit of itself, unless it abides in the vine, so neither [can] you, unless you abide in Me. *5* I am the vine, you are the branches; he who abides in Me, and I in him, he bears much fruit; for apart from Me you can do nothing. *6* **If anyone does not abide in Me, he is thrown away as a branch, and dries up; and**

they gather them, and cast them into the fire, and they are burned. *[This fire is not the lake of fire, but the fire and heat that is going to be prevalent during the bowl judgments].* (italicized words and emphasis added)

Look at Matthew 13:47, another parable that totally aligns with the winnowing that takes place at the sheep and goat judgment on the last day.

Matthew 13:47 Again, the kingdom of heaven is like a dragnet cast into the sea, and gathering [fish] of every kind; *48* and when it was filled they drew it up on the beach; and they sat down, and gathered the good [fish] into containers, *[the sheep]* but the bad they threw away *[the goats]*. *49* So it will be at the end of the age; the angels shall come forth, and take out the wicked from among the righteous *50* and will cast them into the furnace of fire; there shall be weeping and gnashing of teeth.

This furnace of fire, where there is weeping and gnashing of teeth is not the lake of fire, but what the earth will be like during the devastating bowl judgments. We can see this from Malachi 4:1-2.

Malachi 4:1 Surely the day is coming; it will burn like a furnace. All the arrogant and every evildoer will be stubble, and that day that is coming will set them on fire, says the LORD Almighty. Not a root or a branch will be left to them.

Their outcome is exactly what Christ said would happen to all those who did not abide in Him (Jn. 15:6); they would be gathered like a withered branch and burned. It also corresponds with the angels gathering all those who practiced lawlessness and throwing them into the furnace. The timing of its occurrence lines up exactly with what takes place after the sheep and goat judgment, because the seventh trumpet heralds the beginning of the bowl judgments on mankind. It also marks the time for rewards to be given out for those in heaven. Revelation 11:15 shows us exactly what takes place at the seventh trumpet.

Revelation 11:15 And the seventh angel sounded; and there arose loud voices in heaven, saying, 'The kingdom of the world has become [the kingdom] of our Lord, and of His

REVELATION UNRAVELED

Christ; and He will reign forever and ever...' *17* saying, 'We give Thee thanks, O Lord God, the Almighty, who art and who wast, because Thou hast taken Thy great power and hast begun to reign. *18* And the nations were enraged, and Thy wrath came, and the time [came] for the dead to be judged, *[at the Resurrection of the ust]* and [the time] to give their reward to Thy bond-servants the prophets and to the saints and to those who fear Thy name, the small and the great, *[at the judgment seat of Christ]* and to destroy those who destroy the earth.' *[which comes by way of the impending bowl judgments]* (italicized words added)

God will be enacting His judgment on mankind by way of the bowl judgments, while the faithful saints are enjoying being rewarded by Jesus Christ and being a part of the Marriage Supper of the Lamb.

The Bowl Judgments

Having covered what will be taking place in heaven, we can now begin to discover what will be taking place down on earth.

Revelation 16:1 And I heard a loud voice from the temple, saying to the seven angels, 'Go and pour out the seven bowls of the wrath of God into the earth.'

Here we find the last seven plagues are referred to as "bowls," which is the word *shapak*. It is an idiom that is used to connote the speed in which the judgments are executed. Bowls are shallow and quickly dumped, so it is telling us here that these judgments are going to come both rapidly and without mercy.

Revelation 16:2 And the first [angel] went and poured out his bowl into the earth; and it became a loathsome and malignant sore upon the men who had the mark of the beast and who worshiped his image.

The first bowl judgment begins with people getting a grievous sore presumably where they have taken the mark of the beast. I say this because the new implantable bio-chip referred to earlier is powered by a lithium battery and if this battery is tampered with, leaks lithium within the body and causes just what we read here — a malignant sore on the flesh.

> **Revelation 16:3** And the second [angel] poured out his bowl into the sea, and it became blood like [that] of a dead man; and every living thing in the sea died.

The seas will turn into a thick, coagulated mess of blood — a sickening and horrifying sight.

> **Revelation 16:4** And the third [angel] poured out his bowl into the rivers and the springs of waters; and they became blood. *5* And I heard the angel of the waters saying, 'Righteous art Thou, who art and who wast, O Holy One, because Thou didst judge these things; *6* for they poured out the blood of saints and prophets, and Thou hast given them blood to drink. They deserve it.' *7* And I heard the altar saying, 'Yes, O Lord God, the Almighty, true and righteous are Thy judgments.' *8* And the fourth [angel] poured out his bowl upon the sun; and it was given to it to **scorch men with fire. *9* And men were scorched with fierce heat;** and they blasphemed the name of God who has the power over these plagues; and they did not repent, so as to give Him glory. (emphasis added)

We can now see that this scorching heat from the sun is what Jesus was referring to when He cast out the tares into the furnace of fire; for the lake of fire is not started until *after* the Battle of Armageddon and even then *only the beast and the false prophet* are thrown into it. All of unrepentant mankind killed during the bowl judgments will be raised at the resurrection of the unjust that occurs after the 1000 year rule of Christ is over, and *then* they are thrown into the lake of fire — not before.

> **Revelation 16:9** And men were scorched with fierce heat; and they blasphemed the name of God who has the power over these plagues; and they did not repent, so as to give Him glory. *10* And the fifth [angel] poured out his bowl upon the throne of the beast; and his kingdom became darkened; and they gnawed their tongues because of pain,

This shows what Christ meant when He said He would throw the unprofitable servant into *"outer darkness, where there will be weeping and gnashing of teeth."* The sores on people's bodies and the darkness covering the earth will cause them to weep and to gnash their teeth.

The word "gnashing of teeth" comes from the Greek word *brugmos* and it is used to denote extreme anguish and utter despair. It can also be used to describe snarling, or growling, in the sense of biting, which is exactly what the Word says they will be doing to their tongues because of their pain and sores.

The Penalty for Wanton Sin

Now knowing what awaits the "tares" of the kingdom, namely those who decide to renounce Christ and become reprobate, let's confirm further from the epistles that we have to be vigilant in our walk and repent when we go astray.

In 2 Peter, chapter 2, the whole section is speaking of those ministers of the gospel who exploit naive believers into sexual sins, following the way of Balaam. It culminates in verse 20:

> *2 Peter 2:20* For if after they *[these teachers]* have escaped the defilements of the world by the knowledge of the Lord and Savior Jesus Christ, they are again entangled in them and are overcome, the last state has become worse for them than the first. *21* For it would be better for them not to have known the way of righteousness, than having known it, to turn away from the holy commandment delivered to them. *22* It has happened to them according to the true proverb, 'A dog returns to its own vomit,' and, 'A sow, after washing, [returns] to wallowing in the mire.' (italicized words added)

If the Bible says here, and it is in an epistle, that you would be better off *NEVER* to have known the truth than to turn your back on it — how can it be true "once saved, always saved?" That could be the most devastating lie perpetrated on Christendom today because with that false guarantee, many people never really aspire to walk in holiness and obedience because deep down they know it is not necessary — they do not think they can lose it. The Bible says the just shall live *by faith* (Rom. 1:17). We are saved by faith *in* Christ, not a faith that takes place at one moment in your life and can then be forgotten about until the return, but we are to have a *living* faith where Jesus Christ is our Lord and we make Him Lord each and every day of our lives (Heb. 6:11-12).

Abraham is a prime example of what faith is. When he received the promise of God concerning the birth of his son, even though he and Sarah were past child-bearing years, he did not waver in unbelief but *"he grew strong in faith, giving glory to God and being fully persuaded that what God had promised, He was able also to perform. Therefore it was reckoned to him for righteousness."* He believed steadfastly. The connection is then made to us in Romans 4:23.

> ***Romans 4:23*** Now not for his sake only was it written, that it was reckoned to him, ***24*** **but for our sake also, to whom it will be reckoned,** as those who believe in Him who raised Jesus our Lord from the dead, ***25*** [He] who was delivered up because of our transgressions, and was raised because of our justification. (emphasis added)

God wants us to have faith — a faith not based on doing the works of the Law, but instead fueled by an attitude of love and believing in Jesus Christ as the Savior from sin. When one has that kind of attitude and heart for obedience to the Word of God, then good works or fruit will occur naturally in one's life. This truth is made plain in the book of James where it says that faith without works is dead, it is destitute, and will not save you. It says if you walk in faith, works will follow naturally, yet if you have no works; it is an indicator, a barometer, that your faith is dead.

> ***James 2:14*** What use is it, my brethren, if a man says he has faith, but he has no works? Can that faith save him? ***15*** If a brother or sister is without clothing and in need of daily food, ***16*** and one of you says to them, 'Go in peace, be warmed and be filled,' and yet you do not give them what is necessary for [their] body, what use is that? ***17*** Even so faith, if it has no works, is dead, *[nekros, meaning lifeless, destitute]* [being] by itself. ***18*** But someone may [well] say, 'You have faith, and I have works; show me your faith without the works, and I will show you my faith by my works.' ***19*** You believe that God is one. You do well; the demons also believe, and shudder. *[You may believe in God, but that is not enough — the demons even do that. The question is do you have faith, an active faith in God and His promises?]* ***20*** But are you

willing to recognize, you foolish fellow, that faith without works is useless? *21* Was not Abraham our father justified by works, when he offered up Isaac his son on the altar? *22* You see that faith was working with his works, and as a result of the works, faith was perfected; *23* and the Scripture was fulfilled which says, 'And Abraham believed God, and it was reckoned to him as righteousness,' and he was called the friend of God. *24* You see that a man is justified by works, and not by faith alone. *25* And in the same way was not Rahab the harlot also justified by works, when she received the messengers and sent them out by another way? *26* For just as the body without [the] spirit is dead, so also faith without works is dead. (italicized words added)

It is not enough just to mouth allegiance to Christ, but you have to *live it*. Look at Hebrews 10:26...

Hebrews 10:26 For if we go on sinning willfully after receiving the knowledge of the truth, there no longer remains a sacrifice for sins, *27* but a certain terrifying expectation of judgment, and the fury of a fire which will consume the adversaries. *[If we have a guaranteed place in heaven regardless of what we do, why would you have a terrifying expectation of the judgment that will consume the adversaries? The point is if you are willfully walking in sin, you have every reason to fear that fiery judgment]* *28* Anyone who has set aside the Law of Moses dies without mercy on [the testimony of] two or three witnesses. *29* How much severer punishment do you think he will deserve who has trampled underfoot the Son of God, and has regarded as unclean the blood of the covenant by which he was sanctified, and has insulted the Spirit of grace?[45] *30* For we know Him who said, "Vengeance is Mine, I will repay." And again, "The Lord will judge His people." *31* It is a terrifying thing to fall into the hands of the living God. *[Paul then encourages them to get back in line...]* *32* But remember the former days, when, after being enlightened, you endured a great conflict of sufferings, *33* partly, by being made a public spectacle through reproaches and tribulations, and partly by becoming sharers with those who were so treated. *34* For you showed sympathy to the prisoners, and accepted joyfully the seizure of your property, knowing that you have for yourselves a better possession and an abiding one. *35* Therefore, do not throw away your confidence, which has a great reward. *36* For you have need of endurance, so that when you have done the will of God, you may receive what was promised. *37* For yet in a very little while, He who is coming *[Christ]* will come, and will not delay. *38* But My righteous one shall live by faith; And if he shrinks back, My soul has no pleasure in him. *39* But we are not of those who shrink back to destruction, *[Destruction is defined as "utter and final ruin which cannot be reversed" — surely more than the mere losing of rewards]* but of those who have faith to the preserving of the soul. (italicized words and emphasis added)

Galatians 5:16 But I say, walk by the Spirit, and you will not carry out the desire of the flesh. *17* For the flesh sets its desire against the Spirit, and the Spirit against the flesh; for these are in opposition to one another, so that you may not do the things that you please. *18* But if you are led by the Spirit, you are not under the Law. *19* Now the deeds of the flesh are evident, which are: immorality, impurity, sensuality, *20* idolatry, sorcery, enmities, strife, jealousy, outbursts of anger, disputes, dissensions, factions, *21* envying, drunkenness, carousing, and things like these, of which I forewarn you just as I have forewarned you [before] **that those who practice such things shall not inherit the kingdom of God.** (emphasis added)

Paul had to be warning these believers for a reason. Look what Jesus warned His followers about...

Revelation 3:3 Remember therefore what you have received and heard; and keep [it], and repent. If therefore you will not wake up, I will come like a thief, and you will not know at what hour I will come upon you. *4* But you have a few people in Sardis who have not soiled their garments; and they will walk with Me in white; for they are worthy. *5* He who overcomes shall thus be clothed in white garments; **and**

> **I will not ERASE his name from the book of life**,⁴⁶ and I will confess his name before My Father, and before His angels. (emphasis added)

If a "Christian" fails to "overcome" and instead refutes Christ and takes the mark of the beast during the tribulation period he will be damned. To believe anything less is to refute the Word of God. Just read Revelation 14:9-11:

> ***Revelation 14:9*** And another angel, a third one, followed them, saying with a loud voice, 'If **anyone** worships the beast and his image, and receives a mark on his forehead or upon his hand, *10* he also will drink of the wine of the wrath of God, which is mixed in full strength in the cup of His anger; and he will be tormented with fire and brimstone in the presence of the holy angels and in the presence of the Lamb. *11* And the smoke of their torment goes up forever and ever; and they have no rest day and night, those who worship the beast and his image, and **whoever** receives the mark of his name.' (emphasis added)

Though certainly not appealing to what Christians want to think, the Bible says the beast is going to have dominion over the saints living on earth during the tribulation period and they will be faced with this decision — to take the mark of the beast or die. Eternal security and the whole concept that you cannot lose your salvation if you take the mark of the beast is exactly the ploy Satan wants you to fall for — to sell out, to sell your soul for a mess of pottage just like Esau did. Hebrews 12:17 describes what happened to him.

> ***Hebrews 12:17*** For you know that even afterwards, when he desired to inherit the blessing, he was rejected, for he found no place for repentance, though he sought for it with tears.

Christians everywhere have to wake up and see that they need to be faithful in the fight that is approaching!

> ***Galatians 6:7*** Do not be deceived, God is not mocked; for whatever a man sows, this he will also reap. *8* For the one who sows to his own flesh shall from the flesh reap

corruption, but the one who sows to the Spirit shall from the Spirit reap eternal life.

There are only two choices offered here. You either sow to your flesh by going after the things of this world and in turn reap corruption, or you sow to the spirit, by thinking and acting on spiritual principles and as a result reap eternal life.

The Battle of Armageddon

Having covered what takes place in the first five bowl judgments, let us go ahead and pick up in our chronology with the sixth bowl judgment found in Rev. 16:12.

> ***Revelation 16:12*** And the sixth [angel] poured out his bowl upon the great river, the Euphrates; and its water was dried up, that the way might be prepared for the kings from the east. ***13*** And I saw [coming] out of the mouth of the dragon and out of the mouth of the beast and out of the mouth of the false prophet, three unclean spirits like frogs; ***14*** for they are spirits of demons, performing signs, which go out to the kings of the whole world, to gather them together for the war of the great day of God, the Almighty.

God is going to dry up the Euphrates River in order to make easy passage for the armies of the north and the surrounding nations to come down to Jerusalem for war. Powerful demons are going to be at work in the beast and the false prophet (the leader) as they conjure the kings of the whole world to gather for war against God at Armageddon. It is hard to imagine the strength of the deception that will be going on at this point in that man would actually believe he can win a war against God. This kind of blindness is beginning to surface even today as leaders in this country and elsewhere are purposely rejecting, even ridiculing the laws that God set up for man's good.

> ***Revelation 16:15*** Behold, I am coming like a thief. Blessed is the one who stays awake and keeps his clothes, so that he will not walk about naked and men will not see his shame.

I believe Christ injected this admonition right in the middle of this whole distressing scenario as if to tell believers, "Awake! Whatever you do, stay awake and walk in holiness so you will not end up being a part these woes!"

Verse 16 of Revelation 16 tells us that demons gather together the armies of the world at a place called *Armageddon,* which is a Hebrew word that refers to the hill of Megiddo, situated around 55 miles from Jerusalem. It is a hill that overlooks a large valley known as the Valley of Jezreel. This valley is merely going to be a staging area for the world's armies. The real battle will be in the Valley of Jehoshaphat — otherwise known as the Kidron Valley that lies between Jerusalem and the Mount of Olives. We can see this from the book of Joel.

> ***Joel 3:1*** "For behold, in those days and at that time, When I restore the fortunes of Judah and Jerusalem, *2* I will gather all the nations, And bring them down to the valley of Jehoshaphat. Then I will enter into judgment with them there On behalf of My people and My inheritance, Israel, Whom they have scattered among the nations; And they have divided up My land. *[Remember this will be done when the Israelis sign a land for peace agreement known as the covenant with death.]* *12* Let the nations be aroused And come up to the valley of Jehoshaphat, For there I will sit to judge all the surrounding nations. *13* Put in the sickle, for the harvest is ripe. Come, tread, for the wine press is full; The vats overflow, for their wickedness is great. *14* Multitudes, multitudes in the valley of decision! For the day of the LORD is near in the valley of decision. *15* The sun and moon grow dark, And the stars lose their brightness. *16* And the LORD roars from Zion And utters His voice from Jerusalem, And the heavens and the earth tremble. But the LORD is a refuge for His people And a stronghold to the sons of Israel. *17* Then you will know that I am the LORD your God, Dwelling in Zion My holy mountain. So Jerusalem will be holy, And strangers will pass through it no more. (italicized words added)

At the seventh angel, a great earthquake rocks the earth.

> ***Revelation 16:18*** And there were flashes of lightning and sounds and peals of thunder; and there was a great earthquake, such as there had not been since man came to be

upon the earth, so great an earthquake [was it, and] so mighty. *19* And the great city *[New York City]* was split into three parts, and the cities of the nations fell. And Babylon the great was remembered before God, to give her the cup of the wine of His fierce wrath. (italicized words added)

This earthquake will be beyond man's comprehension. Look at Isaiah 24:19.

Isaiah 24:19 The earth is broken asunder, The earth is split through, The earth is shaken violently. *20* The earth reels to and fro like a drunkard, And it totters like a shack, For its transgression is heavy upon it, And it will fall, never to rise again. *21* So it will happen in that day, That the LORD will punish the host of heaven, on high, And the kings of the earth, on earth. *22* And they will be gathered together [like] prisoners in the dungeon, And will be confined in prison; And after many days they will be punished *[which will be at the resurrection of the unjust — 1000 years later]*. (italicized words added)

The destruction of Babylon is spoken of in detail in Revelation 18 which I believe perfectly depicts New York City, when it says *"all the nations have drunk the maddening wine of her adulteries, the kings of the earth committed adultery with her, and the merchants of the earth grew rich from her excessive luxuries."* This modern day Babylon is also called the woman and the harlot in Revelation 17 and the way it is described in the Bible, the other magna-regions that rule with the beast will eventually turn on the woman and make her desolate, which could possibly be some kind of nuclear annihilation of the United States toward the end of the bowl judgments.

What will Armageddon be like? Many Scriptures depict the scene. You have in Revelation 16:21 hailstones weighing 100 pounds each falling on people and in Zechariah 14:12 you have an awesome picture of God's wrath taking place.

Zechariah 14:12 Now this will be the plague with which the LORD will strike all the peoples who have gone to war against Jerusalem; their flesh will rot while they stand on their feet, and their eyes will rot in their sockets, and their tongue will rot in their mouth.

It is easy to see where some movie directors get their ideas. How is the Lord going to do this? He is going to do it with the breath of His mouth, and we are going to be there to watch!

Sometime before the seventh bowl judgment and the Battle of Armageddon occurs, the saints will have finished taking part in the Marriage Supper of the Lamb in heaven which is described in Revelation 19:7. The saints of God then go with Jesus Christ from heaven to wage war against the nations of the earth. We will be the "armies of heaven" that follow Him riding white horses spoken of in Revelation 17:14 as *"those who are with Him are the called, and chosen and faithful."* We will come with Jesus Christ to wage war against the armies of the world!

> ***Revelation 19:11*** And I saw heaven opened; and behold, a white horse, and He who sat upon it [is] called Faithful and True; and in righteousness He judges and wages war. ***12*** And His eyes [are] a flame of fire, and upon His head [are] many diadems; and He has a name written [upon Him] which no one knows except Himself. ***13*** And [He is] clothed with a robe dipped in blood; and His name is called The Word of God. ***14*** And the armies which are in heaven, clothed in fine linen, white [and] clean, were following Him on white horses. ***15*** And from His mouth comes a sharp sword, so that with it He may smite the nations; and He will rule them with a rod of iron; and He treads the wine press of the fierce wrath of God, the Almighty. ***16*** And on His robe and on His thigh He has a name written, "KING OF KINGS, AND LORD OF LORDS." ***17*** And I saw an angel standing in the sun; and he cried out with a loud voice, saying to all the birds which fly in midheaven, 'Come, assemble for the great supper of God; ***18*** in order that you may eat the flesh of kings and the flesh of commanders and the flesh of mighty men and the flesh of horses and of those who sit on them and the flesh of all men, both free men and slaves, and small and great.' ***19*** And I saw the beast and the kings of the earth and their armies, assembled to make war against Him who sat upon the horse, and against His army.

The Chronology of the End Times

Jesus Christ will successfully smite the nations, He being "the stone" that crushes the one-world government, that final kingdom of iron and clay revealed unto Daniel so very long ago. By God's grace and mercy we will be there on the winning side, rejoicing in Christ our Savior.

Timing of the Bowl Judgments and the Restoration of the Earth

Now that we have covered the major portion of the chart, I would like to further define what happens during the 30 and 45 days added on to the 1260 days which make up the last half of the Seventieth Week of Daniel. We know and have covered in detail the events talked about in verses 1-3 of Daniel 12. Daniel then asks in verse 6, *"How long will it be until the **end** of these wonders?"* He was told it will be completed in a time, times, and half a time, or 3 ½ years. Then in verse 8 he asks, *"What will be the **outcome** of these events?"* And the man, dressed in linen, tells Daniel that from the time that the regular sacrifice is abolished and the abomination of desolation is set up there will be 1290 days, or 30 days *more* than the 1260 days of the last half of the Seventieth Week of Daniel. Why is this? It is because the *outcome* of the Seventieth Week will be the duration of the bowl judgments, culminating in Armageddon. Thus by Daniel's added question and the answer given to him, we can conclude that the bowl judgments will last 30 days. Then verse 12...

> ***Daniel 12:12*** How blessed is he who keeps waiting and attains to the 1,335 days!

What is this talking about? 1,335 days is 1290 days + 45 days. What this is most likely referring to is a 45-day time period that God will use in order to restore the earth from the devastation and destruction that occurred during the bowl judgments and make the world ready for the new millennial kingdom. It says "How blessed is he who keeps waiting and attains to the 1335 days!" Why? Because that will be the first day of the Millennium!

To follow along on the chart then, during the 30 days of the bowl judgments, the faithful church is up in heaven getting rewarded at the judgment seat of Christ and taking part in the Marriage Supper of the Lamb. At the end of those 30 days, the elect will return with Christ to deliver judgment against mankind at the Battle of Armageddon. At the end of Armageddon, the beast and the false prophet are thrown into the lake of fire that is created in Edom during the 45-day period of restoration. This is described in Isaiah 34:1-17.

> ***Isaiah 34:1*** Draw near, O nations, to hear; and listen, O peoples! Let the earth and all it contains hear, and the world and all that springs from it. *2* For the LORD'S indignation is against all the nations, And [His] wrath against all their armies; He has utterly destroyed them, *[God is finished with His wrath]* He has given them over to slaughter. *3* So their slain will be thrown out, And their corpses will give off their stench, And the mountains will be drenched with their blood. *4* And all the host of heaven will wear away, And the sky will be rolled up like a scroll; All their hosts will also wither away As a leaf withers from the vine, Or as [one] withers from the fig tree. *5* For My sword is satiated in heaven, Behold it shall descend for judgment upon Edom, And upon the people whom I have devoted to destruction. *6* The sword of the LORD is filled with blood, It is sated with fat, with the blood of lambs and goats, With the fat of the kidneys of rams. For the LORD HAS a sacrifice in Bozrah, And a great slaughter in the land of Edom. *7* Wild oxen shall also fall with them, And young bulls with strong ones; Thus their land shall be soaked with blood, And their dust become greasy with fat. *8* For the LORD has a day of vengeance, A year of recompense for the cause of Zion. *9* And its streams shall be turned into pitch, And its loose earth into brimstone, And its land shall become burning pitch. *10* It shall not be quenched night or day; Its smoke shall go up forever; From generation to generation it shall be desolate; None shall pass through it forever and ever. *[This is the lake of fire]* *11* But pelican and hedgehog shall possess it, And owl and raven shall dwell in it; And He shall stretch over it the line of desolation And the plumb line of emptiness. *12* Its nobles there is no one there [Whom] they may proclaim king — And all its princes shall be nothing. *13* And thorns shall come up in its fortified towers, Nettles and thistles in its fortified cities; It shall also be a haunt of jackals [And] an abode of ostriches. *14* And the desert creatures shall meet with the wolves, The hairy goat also shall cry to its kind;

Yes, the night monster shall settle there And shall find herself a resting place. *15* The tree snake shall make its nest and lay [eggs] there, And it will hatch and gather [them] under its protection. Yes, the hawks shall be gathered there, Every one with its kind. *16* Seek from the book of the LORD, and read: Not one of these will be missing; None will lack its mate. For His mouth has commanded, And His Spirit has gathered them. *17* And He has cast the lot for them, And His hand has divided it to them by line. They shall possess it forever; From generation to generation they shall dwell in it. (italicized words added)

The rest of the dead do not live again until the resurrection of the unjust which occurs when the thousand year reign of Christ is finished, as mentioned in Revelation 20:5. I believe the Word of God states it best...

Revelation 20:7 And when the thousand years are completed, Satan will be released from his prison, *8* and will come out to deceive the nations which are in the four corners of the earth, Gog and Magog, to gather them together for the war; the number of them is like the sand of the seashore. *9* And they came up on the broad plain of the earth and surrounded the camp of the saints and the beloved city, and fire came down from heaven and devoured them. *10* And the devil who deceived them was thrown into the lake of fire and brimstone, where the beast and the false prophet are also; and they will be tormented day and night forever and ever. *11* And I saw a great white throne and Him who sat upon it, from whose presence earth and heaven fled away, and no place was found for them. *12* And I saw the dead, the great and the small, standing before the throne, and books were opened; and another book was opened, which is [the book] of life; and the dead were judged from the things which were written in the books, according to their deeds. *13* And the sea gave up the dead which were in it, and death and Hades gave up the dead which were in them; and they were judged, every one [of them] according to their deeds. *14* And death and Hades were thrown into the lake of fire. This is the second death, the lake of fire. *15* And if anyone's name was not found written in the book of life, he was thrown into the lake of fire.

After all this, Revelation 21:1 says there will be a new heaven and a new earth — and a New Jerusalem.

> ***Revelation 21:1*** And I saw a new heaven and a new earth; for the first heaven and the first earth passed away, and there is no longer [any] sea. *2* And I saw the holy city, New Jerusalem, coming down out of heaven from God, made ready as a bride adorned for her husband. *3* And I heard a loud voice from the throne, saying, 'Behold, the tabernacle of God is among men, and He shall dwell among them, and they shall be His people, and God Himself shall be among them, and He shall wipe away every tear from their eyes; and there shall no longer be [any] death; there shall no longer be [any] mourning, or crying, or pain; the first things have passed away.' *5* And He who sits on the throne said, 'Behold, I am making all things new.' And He said, 'Write, for these words are faithful and true.'

Verse 7 tells us who will be there...

> ***Revelation 21:7*** He who overcomes shall inherit these things, and I will be his God and he will be My son. *8* But for the cowardly and unbelieving and abominable and murderers and immoral persons and sorcerers and idolaters and all liars, their part [will be] in the lake that burns with fire and brimstone, which is the second death.

That is the Word of God my friend. I pray that the teaching of this Word will encourage every one of you to make a decision about what you need to do in order to make sure of your inheritance with the Lord Jesus Christ. The Church needs to repent, to come to grips as to what is at stake as we live our lives here on earth. Are we going to sow to the flesh and reap corruption, or are we going to live as we ought with Christ being our Lord and thus sow to the spirit and as a result reap life everlasting. We will see exactly what the Church needs to repent of as we cover Jesus Christ's message to the seven churches. But let us remember if we obey God's Word, we will live to see the New Jerusalem descend from heaven as described in Revelation 21:10-21 and we will even see the famed streets of gold and gates of pearl. Verses 22 through 27 of chapter 21 tell us more about the wonder and joy that awaits all who prove to be overcomers.

> ***Revelation 21:22*** And I saw no temple therein: for the Lord God Almighty and the Lamb are the temple of it. *23* And the city had no need of the sun, neither of the moon, to shine in it: for the glory of God did lighten it, and the Lamb [is] the light thereof. *24* And the nations of them which are saved shall walk in the light of it: and the kings of the earth do bring their glory and honour into it. *25* And the gates of it shall not be shut at all by day: for there shall be no night there. *26* And they shall bring the glory and honour of the nations into it. *27* And there shall in no wise enter into it any thing that defileth, neither [whatsoever] worketh abomination, or [maketh] a lie: but they which are written in the Lamb's book of life. (KJV)

May God bless you to be a part of the New Jerusalem and His Heavenly Kingdom.

Chapter 7

Christ's Message to the Seven Churches

We have discussed many key events that God says will take place in the world as He brings the present age to a close. Through learning the details of what horrible things await this world, it is important to draw added courage and hope from God that He will take care of us through such difficult times. The subject of how to prepare oneself for the close of the age is addressed to Christians exactly where it should be — in the first three chapters of the book of Revelation. It is in these chapters that God by way of Jesus Christ, lays out with loving admonition the steps that every believer needs to take in order to insure their safe passage through the turbulent waters ahead. Any Christian who begs off these first three chapters as *not* attributable or applicable to himself does so at his own peril for Christ gives fair warning to His church and it is up to them to heed it; He can do no more. And so it is, now that we know *what* we want to be saved from, let us fervently seek *how* we can be saved from it. To hear what Christ says to His church, we begin with Revelation, chapter one, verse one.

> ***Revelation 1:1*** The Revelation of Jesus Christ, which God gave Him to show to His bondservants, the things which must shortly take place; and He sent and communicated [it] by His angel to His bond-servant John...

The word "revelation" is the word *apocalypse,* and it means "an unveiling or disclosure." This disclosure and unveiling of what has previously been hidden was given to Jesus Christ by God, so Jesus could show to His bond-servants what must shortly come to pass. The word used for bond-servant is the Greek word *doulos,* a term used many times in the New Testament to describe committed servants of the Lord. These kinds of servants were meant to be the designated recipients of this vital knowledge because in God's mind it will shortly come to pass. If 2 Peter

3:8 is any indication as to how God views time, you can imagine just how short the time is to the beginning of the Great Tribulation.

> ***Revelation 1:2*** who bore witness to the word of God and to the testimony of Jesus Christ, [even] to all that he saw. *3* Blessed is he who reads and those who hear the words of the prophecy, and heed the things which are written in it; for the time is near.

The Bible says *blessed* are the people who read and hear the words of this prophecy, and the person who heeds what it says. May God have mercy on anyone who would discourage any Christian from reading or applying the book of Revelation to their own life. To do so would be acting in opposition to God's stated will.

> ***Revelation 1:4*** John to the seven churches that are in Asia: Grace to you and peace, from Him who is and who was and who is to come; and from the seven Spirits who are before His throne;

Here we see that this revelation is written to John so that it can in turn be given to the seven churches which are in Asia and it starts off with a familiar greeting we see throughout the epistles, *"Grace to you and peace from Him who is, and who was and who is to come and from the seven spirits who are before His throne."*

> ***Revelation 1:5*** and from Jesus Christ, the faithful witness, the first-born of the dead, and the ruler of the kings of the earth. To Him who loves us, and released us from our sins by His blood, *6* and He has made us [to be] a kingdom, priests to His God and Father; to Him [be] the glory and the dominion forever and ever. Amen.

This introduction makes sense if it is written to Christians, the church, as opposed to believing Jews during the final days as some theologians propound.

> ***Revelation 1:7*** Behold, He is coming with the clouds, and every eye will see Him, even those who pierced Him; and all the tribes of the earth will mourn over Him. Even so. Amen. *8* I am the Alpha and the Omega,' says the Lord God, 'who is and who was and who is to come, the Almighty.' *9* I, John,

> your brother and fellow partaker in the tribulation and kingdom and perseverance [which are] in Jesus, was on the island called Patmos, because of the word of God and the testimony of Jesus.

The Apostle John, the same John who wrote three epistles and the gospel that bears his name, was exiled to the isle of Patmos by the Roman government in 96 AD because of his outspoken views. While stationed on this island, John was taken ahead in time *by revelation* from Jesus Christ in order to see "the Day of the Lord" and the time and events surrounding the end of man's dominion on earth. Who was John told to direct this message to? Jesus told him to write the revelation down and send it to the seven churches which were in Asia.

> ***Revelation 1:11*** saying, 'Write in a book what you see, and send [it] to the seven churches: to Ephesus and to Smyrna and to Pergamum and to Thyatira and to Sardis and to Philadelphia and to Laodicea.'

These churches made up a core of believers located in an area known today as modern day Turkey. The encouragement and admonition that Jesus spoke in these letters was sorely needed because Christians everywhere were struggling against outside paganism, idolatry within their own people, and growing persecution from the Roman government.[47] These kinds of problems, along with the church skidding into internal corruption and heresy, caused many significant "family problems" that needed to be addressed and corrected.

Instead of shoving the reproofs given in the first three chapters off to some misguided churches of a time gone by, we need to realize that much of what Christ spoke applies to today's church as well. Each believer who seeks to read and hear the words of reproof from Christ towards His church must decide if and under what category their own gross neglect lies, and upon discovering these truths, repent and turn away from the behavior which Christ hates.

The Church at Ephesus

> ***Revelation 2:1*** To the angel of the church in Ephesus write: The One who holds the seven stars in His right hand, the One who walks among the seven golden lamp stands, says this:

We find out from Revelation 1:20 what these seven stars and lamp stands are.

> **Revelation 1:20** As for the mystery of the seven stars which you saw in My right hand, and the seven golden lamp stands: the seven stars are the angels of the seven churches, and the seven lamp stands are the seven churches.

This angel of the church of Ephesus says in the next few verses...

> **Revelation 2:2** I know your deeds and your toil and perseverance, and that you cannot endure evil men, and you put to the test those who call themselves apostles, and they are not, and you found them [to be] false; *3* and you have perseverance and have endured for My name's sake, and have not grown weary.

The Lord was pleased that as individuals within the body of Christ, they had works, patience, and as part of their labor they successfully discerned and denounced false apostles within the church body. Who were these false apostles? They were individuals within the body of Christ who rose up and sought to preach a different gospel or a different Jesus other than the one taught by the Apostle Paul. These false apostles, though appearing righteous on the outside, were deceitful workers who will ultimately be recompensed. Paul experienced them among his own people and we are to be on the lookout for them today.

> **Acts 20:28** Be on guard for yourselves and for all the flock, among which the Holy Spirit has made you overseers, to shepherd the church of God which He purchased with His own blood. *29* I know that after my departure savage wolves will come in among you, not sparing the flock; *30* and **from among your own selves men will arise,** speaking perverse things, to draw away the disciples after them. *31* Therefore be on the alert, remembering that night and day for a period of three years I did not cease to admonish each one with tears. (emphasis added)

Even though the believers in Ephesus were able and willing to confront and deal with such spiritual disease within the church, Jesus goes on to tell them in verse 4 of Revelation, chapter 2... *"But I have [this] against you, that you have left your first love."* Evidently, just being spiritually aware does not make one "on fire for the Lord," for Jesus told these followers of Him that they had lost their first love, they had grown cold as to the need and urgency of the gospel. What does Christ say to do?

> ***Revelation 2:5*** Remember therefore from where you have fallen, and repent and do the deeds you did at first; or else I am coming to you, and will remove your lamp stand out of its place - unless you repent.

This is worthy of note. Christ tells this church to repent, to turn away from their fallen practices and come back and do the "first works," that of loving and serving Him with all their hearts. This church was already testing false apostles within their ranks and dealing with those who were causing rifts and bringing false practices within the church yet they were reproved for not serving Christ with the best intentions in mind. Does this tell us anything about what Christ must think about the true state of our churches today? Certainly many must be falling far short of the Lord's expectations. And what did He tell them would happen if they didn't repent? He told them He would remove, shake, the candlestick (the church) out of its place. A holy judgment of unknown consequences will befall sidetracked believers if they fail to get in line.

> ***Revelation 2:6*** Yet this you do have, that you hate the deeds of the Nicolaitans, which I also hate.

Christ does congratulate them on this point — they hate the deeds, the practices of the Nicolaitans. What were these practices? They were those individuals within the church who attempted to recreate the heirarchy of the Old Testament priesthood.[48] By lauding or setting themselves over the laypeople within the church, they began to exercise a "divine authority" that gave them sole right to interpret the Scriptures for other Christians or they became privy to "special privileges" as that due "special men of God." This perversion of what it means to serve as a leader in the body of Christ caused the resurrected Lord to confess he *hated* the deeds of the Nicolaitans. Thus when it comes to seeing men in leadership positions display such behavior, we should hate it also.

> ***Revelation 2:7*** He who has an ear, let him hear what the Spirit says to the churches. To him who overcomes, I will

grant to eat of the tree of life, which is in the Paradise of God.

The overcomer, he who repents and comes back to his first love, Christ, will eat of the tree of life in the paradise of God (Rev. 22:1, 2). The importance of heeding Christ's call to be an overcomer, by being faithful, is a theme we will see is vital to every Christian's future.

The Church of Smyrna

> ***Revelation 2:8*** And to the angel of the church in Smyrna write: The first and the last, who was dead, and has come to life, says this: *9* I know your tribulation and your poverty but you are rich, and the blasphemy by those who say they are Jews and are not, but are a synagogue of Satan. *10* Do not fear what you are about to suffer. Behold, the devil is about to cast some of you into prison, that you may be tested, and you will have tribulation ten days. Be faithful until death, and I will give you the crown of life. *11* He who has an ear, let him hear what the Spirit says to the churches. He who overcomes shall not be hurt by the second death.

What is the second death that the overcomer will avoid? It is to be cast into the lake of fire with the rest of the world's unbelievers.

> ***Revelation 20:14*** And death and Hades were thrown into the lake of fire. This is the second death, the lake of fire.

There is a contingency the believer in Christ must meet to avoid this unthinkable sentence. It is to be faithful to Christ until the end, and the subject of persecution is handled here in the letter to the church in Smyrna. It states emphatically that despite their tribulation and poverty, Christ saw them as rich, being well aware that those who were persecuting them were not true Jews, but instead under the influence and domination of Satan. In regard to their suffering, He encouraged them to do one thing — be faithful unto death and by doing *that* He will gladly reward them with a crown of life and their protection from the second death would be assured. The lesson for today's church is loud and clear. Obedience is more desired by Christ than sacrifice. Though poor in worldly goods, Jesus Christ looked fondly on the steadfast faith of the saints in Smyrna. Will Christ be able to say the same about you and your church when you stand in the face of persecution now and in the future?

The Church of Pergamum

> ***Revelation 2:12*** And to the angel of the church in Pergamum write: The One who has the sharp two-edged sword says this: *13* I know where you dwell, where Satan's throne is; and you hold fast My name, and did not deny My faith, even in the days of Antipas, My witness, My faithful one, who was killed among you, where Satan dwells.

The ancient town of Pergamum, now called Bergama, was located north of Smyrna in the province of Turkey. Pergamum was a city noted for its temples and statues of their pagan gods. Their main god was called Aesculapius, a god of healing, and its symbol was that of a serpent.[49] The image of the serpent used in their worship was even embossed on much of their currency and much of the food entering the city was also sacrificed to pagan gods before being sold in the open markets thus it was extremely hard for Christians to be a part of public festivals and city life with idolatry so prevalent. Despite the spiritually dark conditions, believers stayed true to Christ in Pergamum, even weathering the persecution that arose when Christ's faithful man Antipas was slain in this mecca of Babylonian mystery religion. Perhaps what is most amazing is as admirable as these believers may seem, Christ still took them to task about a point in which he was *not* happy.

> ***Revelation 2:14*** But I have a few things against you, because you have there some who hold the teaching of Balaam, who kept teaching Balak to put a stumbling block before the sons of Israel, to eat things sacrificed to idols, and to commit [acts of] immorality.

The doctrine of Balaam that Christ mentions here refers to the way Israel was seduced into *spiritual* fornication through the introduction of sexual misconduct among its people. To fully understand more about the doctrine of Balaam you need to read the book of Numbers, chapters 22-24. There Balak, the pagan king of Moab, besought Balaam, a corrupted prophet of the Lord, to curse Israel. Though Balaam remained true to the Lord in that he did not utter a curse on the tribes of Israel, he did something just as onerous by telling Balak how to corrupt and destroy the children of Israel from within. Balaam told Balak that the way to weaken Israel was to introduce pagan women into Israel's ranks and through the ravages of sexual license; the men of Israel would corrupt themselves and lose their true spiritual calling. Once Israel was led into physical fornication it would then lead them into spiritual fornication and a turning away of their hearts from God. This form of spiritual trickery, allowing church members to become physical fornicators, yields the same results today as it did in Balaam's time — the church soon finds their members becoming "spiritual harlots" going after other gods, rather than following their true husband — Christ. How does Christ respond to this spiritual harlotry?

> ***Revelation 2:16*** Repent therefore; or else I am coming to you quickly, and I will make war against them with the sword of My mouth.

The Lord will begin to raise His sword against the idolaters and spiritual fornicators within the church and it will begin to happen as the seals of Revelation are opened.

> ***Revelation 2:17*** He who has an ear, let him hear what the Spirit says to the churches. To him who overcomes, to him I will give [some] of the hidden manna, and I will give him a white stone, and a new name written on the stone which no one knows but he who receives it.

Believers who overcome and resist temptations of the flesh will be given "hidden manna" by Christ and receive a "white stone" with a new name written on it. A white stone was commonly used to connote acquittal by juries within ancient courts of law. Thus with beautiful and accurate symbolism, Christ promises a declaration of innocence and a new name for every believer who stays faithful and overcomes the tempting sways within the corrupted church.

The Church of Thyatira

> ***Revelation 2:18*** And to the angel of the church in Thyatira write: The Son of God, who has eyes like a flame of fire, and His feet are like burnished bronze, says this;

This verse parallels the vivid description of Christ given in Revelation 1:13-15, and again shows our resurrected Savior ready for judgment as He seeks to warn and cleanse His church.

> ***Revelation 2:19*** I know your deeds, and your love and faith and service and perseverance, and that your deeds of late are greater than at first. ***20*** But I have [this] against you, that you tolerate the woman Jezebel, who calls herself a prophetess, and she teaches and leads My bond-servants astray, so that they commit [acts of] immorality and eat things sacrificed to idols.

The standard the Lord expects is indeed high. Despite the church of Thyatira's admirable works of charity, faith and patience, Christ let it be known He is not happy with their allowance of false prophets within the church who seduce and lead away His servants to commit fornication and eat things sacrificed unto idols.

Jezebel is mentioned because she was a prime example of spiritual cunning and decadence in the Old Testament. Through her machinations with her husband Ahab, she sought to bring in Baal worship throughout Israel. The phrase "that you tolerate the woman Jezebel" is a metaphor insinuating the church had allowed immorality and idolatry to take hold within the body of believers.

> ***Revelation 2:21*** And I gave her time to repent; and she does not want to repent of her immorality. ***22*** Behold, I will cast her upon a bed [of sickness], and those who commit adultery with her into great tribulation, unless they repent of her deeds. ***23*** And I will kill her children with pestilence; and all the churches will know that I am He who searches the minds and hearts; and I will give to each one of you according to your deeds.

Jesus says here He gave those who followed "Jezebel" ample time to repent and they refused. What is the consequence of such outright rebellion and lasciviousness?

> ***Revelation 2:22*** Behold, I will cast her upon a bed [of sickness], and those who commit adultery with her into great tribulation, unless they repent of her deeds.

Christ is saying to those in the church, who flagrantly disregard His warning; they will be cast into the Great Tribulation.

Revelation 2:23 And I will kill her children with pestilence; and all the churches will know that I am He who searches the minds and hearts; and I will give to each one of you according to your deeds.

Through the massive judgments due to take place upon the unfaithful church during the Great Tribulation, repentant believers will finally realize that the Lord is in the business of searching the reins and motives of people's hearts and through His fiery testing, they will learn to submit and willfully obey the Lord.

Revelation 2:24 But I say to you, the rest who are in Thyatira, who do not hold this teaching, who have not known the deep things of Satan, as they call them — I place no other burden on you. *25* Nevertheless what you have, hold fast until I come.

Those in the church who did not fall prey to the doctrine of Jezebel, but kept themselves pure — Christ lays on them "no other burden," but encourages them to hold fast till He comes, which given their purity of heart, will be at the time of the rapture, which occurs right before the Great Tribulation begins.

Revelation 2:26 And he who overcomes, and he who keeps My deeds until the end, to him I will give authority over the nations; *27* and he shall rule them with a rod of iron, as the vessels of the potter are broken to pieces, as I also have received [authority] from My Father;

Those of the *unfaithful* church who repent and are faithful unto death during the Great Tribulation become what are called "overcomers," and Jesus promises them positions of authority in the Millennium to come. His grace and goodness still reigns to all those who will repent and choose to truly serve Him.

The Church in Sardis

Revelation 3:1 And to the angel of the church in Sardis write: He who has the seven Spirits of God, and the seven stars, says this: 'I know your deeds, that you have a name that you are alive, but you are dead.'

Christ knew that the church at Sardis was esteemed by society as being an alive and vital church, much like many large churches today that boast record numbers both in attendance and numerous programs. But what is Christ's opinion of this "growing" church? It is *"I know your deeds, that you have a name that you are alive, but you are dead."* How could this be? Many Scriptures give us insight as to what can happen inside church circles.

> *1 Timothy 6:3* If anyone advocates a different doctrine, and does not agree with sound words, those of our Lord Jesus Christ, and with the doctrine conforming to godliness, *4* he is conceited *and* understands nothing; but he has a morbid interest in controversial questions and disputes about words, out of which arise envy, strife, abusive language, evil suspicions...

One camp that can arise in the body of Christ are those who become obsessed with "head knowledge" rather than developing a real heart of love and service for God. Another camp includes those who believe in "the prosperity gospel," and begin to equate one's spirituality with the amount of physical possessions they are able to attain as stated in the next verse:

> *I Timothy 6:5* and constant friction between men of depraved mind and deprived of the truth, who suppose that godliness is a means of great gain.

This type of believer can easily fall into the attitudes and behaviors typified by Paul in his second letter to Timothy.

> *2 Timothy 3:1* But realize this, that in the last days difficult times will come. *2* For men will be lovers of self, lovers of money, boastful, arrogant, revilers, disobedient to parents, ungrateful, unholy, *3* unloving, irreconcilable, malicious gossips, without self-control, brutal, haters of good, *4* treacherous, reckless, conceited, lovers of pleasure rather than lovers of God,

The Apostle Paul told Timothy that in the last days all these behaviors would become evident — and much of it can be seen today. Paul then elaborates in verse 5 concerning these people who are lovers of pleasure rather than lovers of God ...

> ***2 Timothy 3:5*** Having a form of godliness, but denying the power thereof: from such turn away. (KJV)

There are evidently people within churches who have a form of godliness but *deny the power thereof.* Godliness here is the Greek word *eusebeia,* which means piety, and it is the same word used in reference to true godliness.[50] These people then are those who look and act righteous on the outside, but in fact "deny the [God's] power," on the inside. They really do not know God. They deny His working, much like when the Pharisees insinuated Christ did miracles by the work of devils.

> ***Matthew 12:24*** But when the Pharisees heard it, they said, 'This man casts out demons only by Beelzebul the ruler of the demons.'

The Pharisees blasted and ridiculed Christ about the source of His power by which He did miracles. Jesus Christ spoke out against their grievous charge.

> ***Matthew 12:31*** Therefore I say to you, any sin and blasphemy shall be forgiven men, but blasphemy against the Spirit shall not be forgiven. ***32*** And whoever shall speak a word against the Son of Man, it shall be forgiven him; but **whoever shall speak against the Holy Spirit, it shall not be forgiven him, either in this age, or in the [age] to come.**

This is happening even today as well meaning religious people denounce the power of God being displayed as tantamount to the devil's working. What happens to these kinds of individuals, who keep up appearances on the outside but deny the power and conviction of the Holy Spirit?

> ***2 Timothy 3:6*** For among them are those who enter into households and captivate weak women weighed down with sins, led on by various impulses, ***7*** always learning and never able to come to the knowledge of the truth. ***8*** And just as Jannes and Jambres opposed Moses, so these [men] also

oppose the truth, men of depraved mind, rejected as regards the faith.

These types of people end up finding themselves getting involved in nefarious acts of sin; all the while keeping up an acceptable front before others. They are called hypocrites. The Pharisees were guilty of this behavior — religious and pious on the outside — but soiled and contaminated within. Jesus spoke out regarding their hypocrisy.

Matthew 6:1 Beware of practicing your righteousness before men to be noticed by them; otherwise you have no reward with your Father who is in heaven. *2* When therefore you give alms, do not sound a trumpet before you, as the hypocrites do in the synagogues and in the streets, that they may be honored by men. Truly I say to you, they have their reward in full. *3* But when you give alms, do not let your left hand know what your right hand is doing *4* that your alms may be in secret; and your Father who sees in secret will repay you. *5* And when you pray, you are not to be as the hypocrites; for they love to stand and pray in the synagogues and on the street comers, in order to be seen by men. Truly I say to you, they have their reward in full.

God is not interested in certain outward displays of righteousness — whether you lift holy hands or not or whether you display and follow through on all the modern trappings of what is expected of believers in popular evangelical or charismatic circles today. God looks on the heart, and cares only if your heart is in love with Him, instead of being overly concerned with what people around you may think. Jesus knows one's true motives and He will be the one who will judge whether our actions are born out of a genuine love for Him or a compelling self-interest to look good in the sight of others. What does He tell us to do?

Revelation 3:2 Wake up, and strengthen the things that remain, which were about to die; for I have not found your deeds completed in the sight of My God. *3* Remember therefore what you have received and heard; and keep [it] and repent. If therefore you will not wake up, I will come like a thief, and you will not know at what hour I will come upon you.

This somber warning to the church in Sardis was needed and is reminiscent of Jesus' warning to His disciples in light of the end times and those anticipating His return.

> ***Matthew 24:42*** Therefore be on the alert, for you do not know which day your Lord is coming. *43* But be sure of this, that if the head of the house had known at what time of the night the thief was coming, he would have been on the alert and would not have allowed his house to be broken into. *44* For this reason you be ready too; for the Son of Man is coming at an hour when you do not think [He will.]

Hypocritical Christians, those who remain spiritually "asleep at the switch," will find themselves cast into the throes of the Great Tribulation and will not be part of the rapture. Listen to the contrast in the comfort given to the watchful and spiritually awake church of the Thessalonians.

> ***1 Thessalonians 5:1*** Now as to the times and the epochs, brethren, you have no need of anything to be written to you. *2* For you yourselves know full well that the day of the Lord will come just like a thief in the night. *3* While they are saying, "Peace and safety!" then destruction will come upon them suddenly like birth pangs upon a woman with child; and they shall not escape. *4* But you, brethren, are not in darkness, that the day should overtake you like a thief; *5* for you are all sons of light and sons of day. We are not of night nor of darkness; *6* so then let us not sleep as others do, but let us be alert and sober. *9* For God has not destined us for wrath, but for obtaining salvation through our Lord Jesus Christ, *10* who died for us, that whether we are awake or asleep, we may live together with Him. *11* Therefore encourage one another, and build up one another, just as you also are doing.

The church of Thessalonica was a church spiritually on fire and fervently anticipating the Lord's return. They were like the few in Sardis who had kept their eyes on the Lord Jesus Christ.

> ***Revelation 3:4*** But you have a few people in Sardis who have not soiled their garments; and they will walk with Me in white; for they are worthy.

These select few in Sardis were staying their minds and hearts on practicing the Word of God, being faithful to their Savior, and awaiting His return. To those who have to endure the lessons and tests of the Great Tribulation, Christ says...

> ***Revelation 3:5*** He who overcomes shall thus be clothed in white garments; and I will not erase his name from the book of life, and I will confess his name before My Father, and before His angels.

At what point in time is He talking about? He is talking about the end of the Great Tribulation which closes out the Seventieth Week of Daniel and concludes with the resurrection of the just. If the wayward believers of the Sardis church "overcome" by staying faithful unto death, Jesus says He will *not* blot out their name from the book of life. However, the all important truth remains that if they *do not* overcome the fiery testing of the tribulation period and instead sell out to the world by taking the mark of the beast, Christ *will* blot their name out of the book of life.

> ***Revelation 14:9*** And another angel, a third one, followed them, saying with a loud voice, 'If anyone worships the beast and his image, and receives a mark on his forehead or upon his hand, ***10*** he also will drink of the wine of the wrath of God, which is mixed in full strength in the cup of His anger; and he will be tormented with fire and brimstone in the presence of the holy angels and in the presence of the Lamb. ***11*** And the smoke of their torment goes up forever and ever; and they have no rest day and night, those who worship the beast and his image, and whoever receives the mark of his name.' ***12*** Here is the perseverance of the saints who keep the commandments of God and their faith in Jesus.

> ***Revelation 15:2*** And I saw, as it were, a sea of glass mixed with fire, and those who had come off victorious from the beast and from his image and from the number of his name, standing on the sea of glass, holding harps of God.

> ***Revelation 20:4*** And I saw thrones, and they sat upon them, and judgment was given to them. And I [saw] the souls of those who had been beheaded because of the testimony of

Jesus and because of the word of God, and those who had not worshiped the beast or his image, and had not received the mark upon their forehead and upon their hand; and they came to life and reigned with Christ for a thousand years.

The Great Tribulation will serve as the ultimate proving ground for compromising and unfaithful believers to show whether they want to live for Christ or not. That is why the book of Revelation is written, to warn the churches what they must do to get themselves ready for the righteous Master's return.

The Church in Philadelphia

We now move to the church of Philadelphia which was given a promise that every believer should strive to attain.

> ***Revelation 3:7*** And to the angel of the church in Philadelphia write: He who is holy, who is true, who has the key of David, who opens and no one will shut, and who shuts and no one opens, says this: *8* 'I know your deeds. Behold, I have put before you an open door which no one can shut, because you have a little power, and have kept My word, and have not denied My name.'

This church of "little strength," that had been faithful in keeping Christ's word and not denying His name, was told there was an open door set before them which no man could shut. What is this door? I believe it signifies the rapture, that door of escape for the church by which every faithful believer will be rescued out of the dark days of the Great Tribulation. Why were they spared going through the tribulation? Because they had already proven themselves true and faithful. Jesus says this in verse ten.

> ***Revelation 3:10*** Because you have kept the word of My perseverance, I also will keep you from the hour of testing, that [hour] which is about to come upon the whole world, to test those who dwell upon the earth.

Jesus says He will keep and guard the faithful believer from the hour of testing. The word "testing" comes from the Greek word *peirazo*, which means "to make proof of, test, tempt" and it is derived from the word *peira* which means "a trial, an experiment." This is the same word used in Revelation 2:2 where it says the church of Ephesus put to the test those who called themselves apostles but in reality, were not. This word then provides wonderful insight. The testing of the Great Tribulation will be the means whereby the genuineness of a person's "Christian" belief will be made known.

The word "from" in the phrase *"I will keep them from the hour of testing"* is the word *ek* which means "out from within." Jesus Christ will keep the faithful believer "out from within" the ravages of the tribulation by way of the rapture. First Thessalonians 1:10, speaking to the faithful Thessalonians says it another way.

> **1 Thessalonians 1:10** And [how you] look forward to and await the coming of His Son from heaven, Whom He raised from the dead, Jesus Who personally **rescues** and delivers us out of and from the wrath [bringing punishment] which is coming upon the impenitent and draws us to Himself [that is, invests us with all the privileges and rewards of the new life in Christ, the Messiah]. (Amplified Bible) (emphasis added)

The word "rescue" in this verse is the word *rhuomai* which means "to draw to one's self, to deliver." This apt description of the rapture coincides perfectly with the timing of the saints being seen in heaven at the opening of the fifth seal. The raptured saints spoken about in Revelation 7:13-14 further establishes the truth that these particular saints are rescued out of the Great Tribulation because of their faithfulness.

> **Revelation 3:11** I am coming quickly; hold fast what you have, in order that no one take your crown.

The encouragement that Christ leaves with the church of Philadelphia, and all those who are faithful to Him is *"hold fast what you have* [your testimony] *in order that no one take your crown* [cause you to lose your rewards]." Jesus gives His faithful brethren another promise that is beautiful and worth paying the ultimate sacrifice for.

> **Revelation 3:12** He who overcomes, I will make him a pillar in the temple of My God, and he will not go out from it anymore; and I will write upon him the name of My God, and the name of the city of My God, the new Jerusalem, which

comes down out of heaven from My God, and My new name.

Contrary to those people who will be deceived into taking the mark of the beast on their hand or forehead during the Great Tribulation (Rev. 13:16), Jesus says He will put the name of the Lord on all the foreheads of those faithful to Him. (Rev. 22:4-5)

The Church in Laodicea

The last of the seven churches is the church of the Laodiceans.

> ***Revelation 3:14*** And to the angel of the church in Laodicea write: The Amen, the faithful and true Witness, the Beginning of the creation of God, says this: ***15*** I know your deeds, that you are neither cold nor hot; I would that you were cold or hot. ***16*** So because you are lukewarm, and neither hot nor cold, I will spit you out of My mouth. ***17*** Because you say, 'I am rich, and have become wealthy, and have need of nothing,' and you do not know that you are wretched and miserable and poor and blind and naked,

Laodicea was a rich commercial center that thrived especially during the times of the Romans. Banking and exchange, along with producing such specialty products as black wool, medicinal tablets and powders, made this a prosperous city well known throughout Asia. Yet for all of their wealth, the Lord had strong admonition concerning their lifestyle and spiritual state. He said they were neither cold or hot — but lukewarm to the things of God, and because of their spiritual malaise, Christ said He would reject them.

> ***Revelation 3:15*** I know your deeds, that you are neither cold nor hot; I would that you were cold or hot. ***16*** So because you are lukewarm, and neither hot nor cold, I will spit you out of My mouth.

How did the Laodiceans get into such a state of atrophy?

> ***Revelation 3:17*** Because you say, 'I am rich, and have become wealthy, and have need of nothing,' and you do not know that you are wretched and miserable and poor and blind and naked,

What does He give them for advice?

> *18* I advise you to buy from Me gold refined by fire, that you may become rich, and white garments, that you may clothe yourself, and [that] the shame of your nakedness may not be revealed; and eye salve to anoint your eyes, that you may see.

Christ encouraged the church in Laodicea to pursue things pertaining to the kingdom of God, for in doing this, He could insure them riches that could not be destroyed by the fire of judgment, for it would be built upon obedience to the Word of God. By doing this, they would be clothed with the white raiment that the faithful in Christ already enjoy.

It is critical for Christians today to understand the implications of Christ's reproofs to this church. Today, church members tend to look on the size and beauty of one's sanctuary as indicative of God's blessing on that place or congregation. This could be a completely erroneous assumption, for such a church could be a carbon copy of the church at Laodecia, "increased with goods and in need of nothing" yet be as Christ said, "wretched and miserable and poor and blind and naked." Is this to say Christians should take a vow of poverty and renounce all of their worldly goods? No, but the Bible *does* explicitly warn about the subtle deceptions that can occur when believers take their eyes off God and instead fasten them on riches and the things of this world.

> *1 Timothy 6:9* But those who want to get rich fall into temptation and a snare and many foolish and harmful desires which plunge men into ruin and destruction. *10* For the love of money is a root of all sorts of evil, and some by longing for it have wandered away from the faith, and pierced themselves with many a pang.

The prestige and the accolades the world gives people of wealth can lead a believer down a slippery slope of lies and spiritual compromise. What does the Word of God say the balance is?

> *1 Timothy 6:6* But godliness [actually] is a means of great gain, when accompanied by contentment. *7* For we have brought nothing into the world, so we cannot take anything out of it either. *8* And if we have food and covering, with these we shall be content.

When we trust in God, rather than riches, then our spiritual priorities will be in order.

> *1 Timothy 6:17* Instruct those who are rich in this present world not to be conceited or to fix their hope on the uncertainty of riches, but on God, who richly supplies us with all things to enjoy. *18* [Instruct them] to do good, to be rich in good works, to be generous and ready to share, *19* storing up for themselves the treasure of a good foundation for the future, so that they may take hold of that which is life indeed.

Could it be that the Laodicean church is addressed last for the very reason that if there ever was a church that mirrors many of the today's churches in the United States, it is the Laodiceans? Resplendent with all the engaging music, comfortable surroundings and fine-tuned messages, every believer in Christ must ask themselves the question, "Are Jesus Christ's words first and foremost in this place of worship?" If they are, praise God and glorify His name. If not, and your congregation's "thermostat" is set on lukewarm, then examine yourself and your doctrine before it is too late. The words of Christ have been spoken, the reproof has been made, and it is now up to the church to carry out the admonition spoken of in the book of Revelation. We would do well to take heed to these Scriptures.

> *Mark 4:18* And others are the ones on whom seed was sown among the thorns; these are the ones who have heard the word, 19 and the worries of the world, and the deceitfulness of riches, and the desires for other things enter in and choke the word, and it becomes unfruitful.

> *1 Corinthians 3:10* According to the grace of God which was given to me, as a wise master builder I laid a foundation, and another is building upon it. But let each man be careful how he builds upon it. *11* For no man can lay a foundation other than the one which is laid, which is Jesus Christ. *12* Now if any man builds upon the foundation with gold, silver, precious stones, wood, hay, straw, *13* each man's work will become evident; for the day will show it, because it is [to be] revealed with fire; and the fire itself will test the quality of each man's work.

James 4:4 You adulteresses, do you not know that friendship with the world is hostility toward God? Therefore whoever wishes to be a friend of the world makes himself an enemy of God.

1 John 2:15 Do not love the world, nor the things in the world. If anyone loves the world, the love of the Father is not in him. *16* For all that is in the world, the lust of the flesh and the lust of the eyes and the boastful pride of life, is not from the Father, but is from the world. *17* And the world is passing away, and [also] its lusts; but the one who does the will of God abides forever.

May God instruct *you* as you seek the Lord's will regarding Christ's message to the seven churches.

Epilogue

Without a doubt we are living in the greatest time in history for we stand at the threshold of the Lord's return. For the alive Christian, this means experiencing the joy and indescribable miracle of being "changed" and seeing our mortal bodies made immortal "in a moment, in the twinkling of an eye."

For those of you reading this book who have not made Jesus Christ Lord of your life, you face a different future. A future that contains no hope, only the nightmare that God says will happen in the days ahead. By God's grace, you have been warned of what Jesus Christ expects of those who follow Him as the days of sorrow draw near. Will you humble yourself and fall at the Master's feet and seek repentance for your sins before it is too late?

To repent means "to turn away from," in essence it means to recognize where you are going wrong and then make a decision to change, to go in the right direction, the way of righteousness. This is done by accepting what Jesus Christ accomplished on the cross through His death and resurrection. He paid the penalty for the sins of mankind so that we could stand approved before a righteous God. This gift of salvation and forgiving grace is attained by doing one thing — believing in the Lord Jesus Christ and making Him Lord of your life.

> **Romans 10:9** that if you confess with your mouth Jesus as Lord, and believe in your heart that God raised Him from the dead, you shall be saved; **10** for with the heart man believes, resulting in righteousness, and with the mouth he confesses, resulting in salvation.

If you will do this simple, yet heartfelt act, God will save you and wash you of your sins. What does God then expect you to do upon making this all-important decision? Love Him, serve Him, and in turn, serve others. This is the road to life everlasting.

My prayer to all who read this book is that you will make that decision and make it soon, for the time is at hand. Repent and be saved so that the God of Heaven may spare you from the wrath to come.

ard
REVELATION UNRAVELED

APPENDIX

The UPC Product Code

Figure 1

All the marks, or bars, in the UPC at left are identified by numbers at the bottom of the code except the three marks at the far left, the middle, and the far right. These remain unidentified.

Figure 2

The three marks that were unidentified in Figure 1 are now isolated.

Figure 3

The three unidentified marks match with the mark design for the number "6". In every barcode there are always three unidentified ones, and they always are the number "6".

Figure 4

Here is the most commonly used design, showing "6" as the accurate numerical value on the left, in the center, and on the right. These three marks again, would be unidentified on the package of your product.

Figure 5

This is the second most commonly seen Universal Product Code. As before, there are three marks which are not identified.

* Thanks to *Last Days in America*, by Bob Fraley for the insights gained in this subject area.

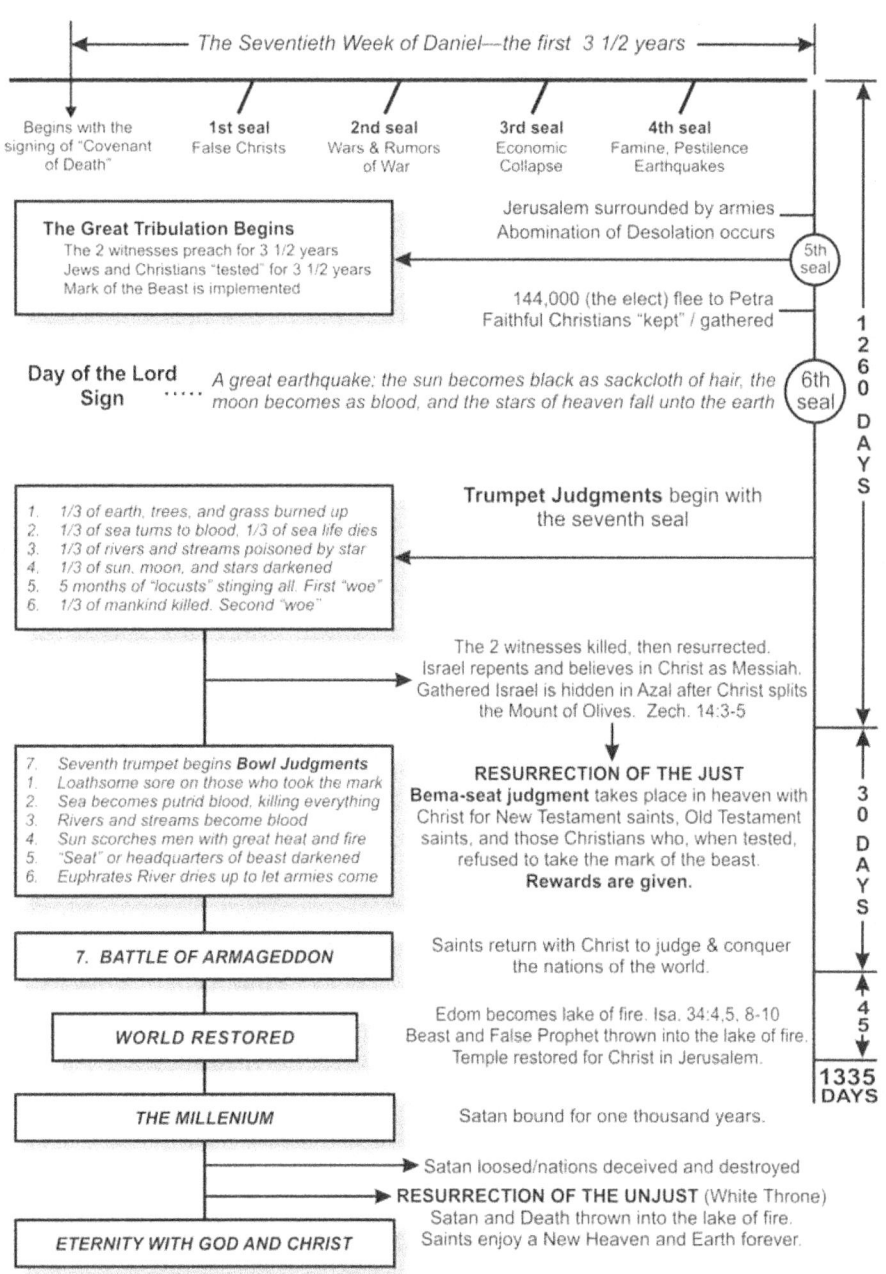

End Times Chronology

1. Signing of the "Covenant of Death." Isa. 28:15,18; Dan. 9:27
2. Seventieth Week of Daniel begins.
3. Next 3 ½ years the first four seals of Revelation are opened. Matt. 24:3-8; Mk. 13:4-8; Rev. 6:1-8
4. Abomination of desolation takes place. Matt. 24:15-22; Mk. 13:14-20; Luke 17:26-30; Luke 21:20-22
5. Great Tribulation begins. Dan. 11:45; Dan. 12:1; Rev. 6:9-11; Rev. 12:6-17; Matt. 24:21; Mk. 13:19
6. The remnant of 144,000 Jews flee to the wilderness (Edom) for the next 3 ½ years to be protected by God. Rev. 12:6; Dan. 12:1; Ps. 91
7. True believers supernaturally kept from harm during this time by way of the rapture. Rev. 3:10; Matt. 24:22; Lk. 21:34-36; Lk. 17:29; Lk. 17:32-37
8. Carnal believers refined, purged. Jer. 30:11,14,15; Rev. 17:12-14
9. One-world government implemented. Rev. 13:6,7,16; Rev. 17:12-14
10. Economic control in place via mark of the beast. Rev. 13:16-17
11. Two witnesses preaching with signs following during this final 3 ½ years. Rev. 11:3-6
12. Sixth seal sign appears — the Day of the Lord begins with the trumpet judgments. Rev. 6:12-17; Rev. 8:1-2
13. The 144,000 faithful remnant of Jews sealed on forehead for protection. Rev. 7:3-4
14. Trumpet judgments on the whole earth. Ezek. 7:2-3; Rev. 8:6-13; Rev. 9:1-21
15. The 144,000 Jews gather to Mount Zion along with now repentant Israel just prior to the bowl judgments beginning at the 7th trumpet. Christ splits apart the Mount of Olives for them to flee and be protected in a secret place called Azal away from the ultimate wrath of Almighty God. Zech. 12:9-10; Zech. 14:3-5; Zeph. 3:17-20; Nahum 1:12-13
16. The two witnesses are raised from the dead by God, and are caught up to heaven at the same time of the resurrection of the just. Rev. 11:11-13

17. The "just" (resurrected martyrs and Old Testament saints) are resurrected at "the last day" of the Seventieth Week of Daniel. Dan. 12:2,7; Rev. 11:12-18; Rev. 15:2; Matt. 25:31-46; Lk. 14:14
18. Judgment seat of Christ takes place for Christians, martyrs, and Old Testament saints. Rewards are given. Rev. 11:18
19. Bowl judgments begin on unrepentant mankind. Rev. 16:1-2
20. Bowl judgments culminate in Armageddon (30 days in duration). Dan. 12:11
21. Christ returns in glory with His saints at Armageddon to defeat the armies of the world at the 7th bowl judgment. Rev. 17:14; Rev. 19:11-21
22. Lake of fire is formed in Edom. Is. 34:4,5,8-10
23. The beast and the false prophet are thrown into the lake of fire.
24. 45-day restoration period to prepare for the Millennium. Satan is bound for 1000 years. Dan. 12:12; Rev. 20:2-3
25. Millennium begins — Christ rules the nations for 1000 years. Rev. 20:3-6
26. Satan unloosed again for a season. Rev. 20:7
27. Those deceived by Satan come up against Jerusalem and are destroyed by fire from heaven. Rev. 20:8,10
28. Satan thrown into the lake of fire. Death and hell destroyed. Rev. 20:10, 13-15
29. White Throne Judgment. Rev. 20:11-15. The second death.
30. Eternity begins. Rev. 21:1-27; Rev. 22:1-5

ENDNOTES

Chapter 1 - The Origin and Identity of the Beast

[1] H. Gratton Guiness, *The Divine Program of the World's History* (as quoted in Bible Readings for the Home," Review and Herald Pub. Assoc. London, MCMXLII) 216, 217 and 318-321.

[2] Bob Fraley, *Last Days in America* (Phoenix, AZ: Christian Life Services, 1984) 158

[3] Fraley, 164

[4] John McManus, *The Insiders* (Appleton, John Birch Society, 1995) 69. Quote from "Notable and Quotable," *Wall Street Journal*, April 10, 1991.

[5] Norman Dodd in letter to Howard E. Kershner, December 29, 1962.

[6] "Redefining Law and Order,", *The New American*, 4 Apr. 1994: 71

[7] Marx and Engels, *The Communist Manifesto*, Henry Regnery Co., Chicago, 1954

Chapter 2 - The Mark of the Beast

[8] Bob Fraley, *Last Days in America* (Phoenix, AZ: Christian Life Services, 1984)

[9] Jim Nelson Black, *When Nations Die*, Tyndale House Pub., Wheaton, IL pg. 160

[10] Black, 165-166

[11] Fraley, 266

[12] Since the writing of this book in 1996, technology has only gotten us closer to this scenario. *Applied Digital Solutions* has the patent to the VeriChip,™ which is the implantable RFID (radio frequency identification device) microchip. The company recently bought eXI Wireless that developed Thermo Life™ technology which can convert temperature change into electricity. Using this technology and having the microchip inserted in the back of the hand or in the forehead which is most subject to temperature change, the VeriChip transceiver can be supplied with unlimited power.

Chapter 3 - The Seventy Weeks of Daniel

[13] *New American Standard Exhaustive Concordance* #7620

[14] All definitions from *Strong's Exhaustive Concordance*

[15] First identified in Sir Robert Anderson's *The Coming Prince* (1894)

[16] Missler, Chuck, *Daniel's 70 Weeks*, Koinomia House, 1993. This figure is attained by 445 B.C. – 32 A.D. (476 x 365) = 173,740 days. Add another 24 days for March 14th – April 6th. (April 6th, 32 A.D. being the time Jesus presented Himself as King), and then add another 116 days to account for leap years.

[17] William Jasper, *The Mideast Peace Charade*, The New American, 18 Oct. 1993: 7

[18] Ezek. 44:9 "No foreigner, uncircumcised in heart and uncircumcised in flesh, of all the foreigners who are among the sons of Israel, shall enter my sanctuary."
[19] Isa. 10:21-25; Isa. 48:10; Isa. 54:7-8
[20] Rev. 7:4-8; Rev.14:3-5
[21] Ps. 91; Ps. 27:5; Zeph. 2:2-3
[22] E.W. Bullinger, *The Companion Bible*, (London: Samuel Bagster and Sons) Appendix vii.149
[23] Luke 12:35-48; Matt. 22:3-14; Matt. 18:22-35

Chapter 4 - The Man of Sin Revealed

[24] Strong's Concordance, #444
[25] Ibid., #266

Chapter 5 - A Comparison of the Words of Christ

[26] Strict dispensationalists follow in the footsteps of John Nelson Darby, who departed from the historic faith of the Church and compartmentalized the Scriptures, suggesting that they refer to two disassociated groups of people, Israel, and the Church. (*The Gospel According to Dispentsationalism*, Reginald C. Kimbro, Wittenburg Pub., Toronto, Canada, pg. 9)
[27] Matt. 12:36; Jn. 5:22; Acts 17:31; Rom. 2:16
[28] Mk. 16:20; Acts 2:42-43
[29] Jn. 8:26,28; Jn. 12:50; Jn. 14:10
[30] Ps. 36:1-4
[31] "Seals" are the term used for the first seven judgments of God initiated by the opening of a scroll by Jesus Christ.
[32] William F. Jasper, "Global Gorby," *The New American*, 30 Oct. 1995: 29
[33] Read Rev. 18 for a description of the destruction of Babylon, the United States of America.
[34] Rev. 6:8
[35] For detailed analysis of these events see Larry Burkett, *The Coming Economic Earthquake* (Moody Press) pg. 70-81
[36] G. Edward Griffin, *The Creature from Jekyll Island*, (Appleton: American Opinion 1994) 494-500
[37] *Behold A Pale Horse*, pg. 123
[38] *Final Warning*, pg. 90
[39] Ibid. pg. 91. According to the October 26th issue of *The Gun Owners*, published by Gun Owners of America (GOA), "...the Justice Department has given a generous grant to computer programmers at Carnegie Mellon University to develop a pilot program for registering gun owners." The project will use computers to

amass data on gun owners from their firearm purchases , permits for carrying their weapons, and application for dealer licenses. According to GOA there are plans to integrate the Carnegie Mellon system "with technology allowing police to print out detailed maps locating gun owners on any given street" and to pinpoint gun owners "based on the type of guns they own." Through this system, police or government officials could "easily locate and confiscate those firearms." (cited from *The New American Magazine*, Jan. 8, 1996, pg. 40 *Registration Scheme*.)

40 *The New American*, "Explosive Evidence of a Cover-up" (Aug. 7, 1195) pg. 4 and *The New American*, Prior Knowledge" (Dec. 11,1995) pg. 5.

Chapter 6 - The Chronology of the End Times

41 Rom. 11:25,26; Zech. 13:9; Ezek. 20:21-23; Ezek. 11:17-21; Ezek. 37:21-28.
42 Isa. 54:7,8; Jer.30:14,15; Isa. 10:5,6
43 Ezek. 37:24-28; Isa. 59:17-21; Joel 2:18-19; Isa. 10:20-27; Jer. 30:16-17.
44 Rev. 11:18; Rev. 14:14-19.
45 Malachi 3:5 "So will I come near to you for judgment. I will be quick to testify against sorcerers, adulterers and perjurers, against those who defraud laborers of their wages, who oppress the widows and the fatherless, and deprive aliens of justice, but do not fear me, says the LORD Almighty."
46 The distinction of who will be in the book of life can be seen in Mal. 3:16-18. "Then those who feared the Lord talked with each other, and the Lord listened and heard. A scroll of remembrance was written in his presence concerning those who feared the Lord and who honored His name. They will be mine, says the Lord Almighty, "in the day that I make up my treasured possession. I will spare them, just as in compassion a man spares his son who serves him. And you will again see the distinction between the righteous and the wicked, between those who serve God and those who do not."

Chapter 7 - Christ's Message to the Seven Churches

47 Grant Jeffrey, *Apocalypse, The Coming Judgment of the Nations* (Frontier Research Publications, 1992), pg 59.
48 Ibid. pg. 63
49 Ibid. pg. 68
50 1 Tim. 2:2; 1 Tim. 2:10; 1 Tim. 3:16; 1 Tim. 4:7; 1 Tim. 6:3,6; 2 Pet. 1:3,6,7; 2 Pet. 3:11

www.ingramcontent.com/pod-product-compliance
Lightning Source LLC
Chambersburg PA
CBHW061645040426
42446CB00010B/1587